War & Peace

Ethics Study Guide

Jonathan Rowe

First published 2013

by PushMe Press

Mid Somerset House, Southover, Wells, Somerset BA5 1UH

www.pushmepress.com

© 2014 Inducit Learning Ltd

The right of Jonathan Rowe to be identified as author of this work has been asserted by him in accordance with sections 77 and 78 of the Copyright, Designs and Patents Act 1988.

British Library Cataloguing in Publication Data
A catalogue record for this book is available from the British Library

ISBN: 978-1-909618-32-9 (pbk)
ISBN: 978-1-909618-33-6 (ebk)
ISBN: 978-1-78484-020-4 (hbk)
ISBN: 978-1-910252-43-7 (pdf)

Typeset in Frutiger by booksellerate.com
Printed by Lightning Source

A rich and engaging community assisted by the best teachers in Ethics

ethics.pushmepress.com

Students and teachers explore Ethics through handouts, film clips, presentations, case studies, extracts, games and academic articles.

Pitched just right, and so much more than a textbook, here is a place to engage with critical reflection whatever your level. Marked student essays are also posted.

Contents

Introduction

"War - what's it good for?" asked Edwin Starr, before deciding, "Absolutely nothing!"

This song was a big hit in 1970 and reflected young people's feelings about the Vietnam War. More generally, the 1960s saw a huge change in public attitudes about war, away from the view that it was a patriotic duty and a moral cause towards the view that it was a great evil that accomplished nothing. The "Anti-War Movement" was born. Other similarly themed hits of the 1960s and 1970s were Bob Dylan's Blowin' in the Wind (1963), For What It's Worth by Buffalo Springfield, Give Peace a Chance by the Plastic Ono Band (1969) and John Lennon's Imagine (1971).

Despite all this, war is still with us and it's still entertainment. War-themed movies are hugely popular, whether they are set in our world (Saving Private Ryan, Valkyrie, Inglourious Basterds) or another (Star Wars, The Lord of the Rings, Avatar) and the Call of Duty series shows how popular war-themed games are. In these films and games, war is a good cause, those who fight in it are struggling bravely against evil and war casualties are a noble sacrifice.

The Anti-War Movement hasn't gone away. The "Stop The War Coalition" helped organise a protest in 2002 that involved nearly a million people marching through London to protest the war in Iraq.

As part of an A-Level course, you will need to understand Just War Theory, working from Augustine's and Aquinas' approaches to Just War and other attempts to refine the theory. You should apply it to recent or contemporary wars in order to identify its strengths and weaknesses.

Religious responses to modern warfare may lead you to consider whether religion can ever justify war. You will also examine different motivations for Pacifism, such as following the teaching of Jesus.

War

EVALUATING WAR AND PEACE

To evaluate ideas about war and peace we will look at them from four perspectives, which spell out the acronym **DATA**:

- **DEONTOLOGICAL** - This is the idea that morality is about obeying rules and following duties (deon is the Greek word for duty). Do people have a duty to fight for their country? Is there a moral rule that forbids killing people?

- **AGAPEIC** - This is the idea that morality is about having a good motivation, such as acting on selfless love (agape is the Greek word for selfless love). It is sometimes called Situationism. Can you love your enemy while you are trying to kill them? Is war always about hate?

- **TELEOLOGICAL** - This is the idea that morality is about bringing about the best consequences (telos is the Greek word for goal or purpose). Can war sometimes be a means to an end? Does violence always lead to more violence?

- **ARETAEIC** - This is the idea that morality is about perfecting your character (arete is the Greek word for virtue or excellence). It is sometimes called Virtue Ethics. Does war help build a noble character? Would a good person always prefer a peaceful solution?

IT'S ALL GREEK TO ME

If you find the technical Greek terms off-putting, you might prefer the acronym **RICE**:

- **RULES** - Deontological ethics often presents morality in terms of rules to be obeyed.

- **INTENTIONS** - Agapeic ethics focuses on your intentions rather than your actions.

- **CONSEQUENCES** - Teleological ethics is often known as Consequentialism.

- **EXCELLENCE** - Arete translates as "excellence", and Aretaeic ethics are about trying to promote excellence in yourself and in society.

WHAT DO WE MAKE OF WAR AND PEACE?

How can "war" be an ethical dilemma? Surely it's just wrong? A glance back through history shows how complicated this topic is. In the ancient and medieval worlds, war was considered an honourable and attractive activity, something that "made a man out of you" and showed all the finest qualities of human beings in their best light. For example, the Roman poet Horace wrote in 13 BC:

> *"Dulce et decorum est pro patria mori" - It is a sweet and beautiful thing to die for your homeland.*

Horace wasn't being ironic - this is a widespread belief. Many ancient leaders attracted fame and glory through being victorious in war; Alexander of Macedon (4th C BCE) became "Alexander the Great" because of an aggressive eight-year war of conquest that took his armies through Turkey and Egypt, across Iraq and Iran and down through Afghanistan into northern India. This was history's first war of annihilation and it is estimated that at least 200,000 soldiers died in his battles and a quarter of a million civilians were massacred in captured cities. Yet ancient historians looked back on Alexander as one of the greatest human beings who ever lived.

This attitude to war was just as common in the European Middle Ages, where warfare was a way of life for people born to be knights. This way of thinking is summed up by William Shakespeare in Henry V, where King Henry gives a speech to his troops on St Crispin's Day, right before the Battle of Agincourt:

This story shall the good man teach his son;

And Crispin Crispian shall ne'er go by,

From this day to the ending of the world,

But we in it shall be remember'd;

We few, we happy few, we band of brothers;

For he to-day that sheds his blood with me

Shall be my brother; be he ne'er so vile,

This day shall gentle his condition:

And gentlemen in England now a-bed

Shall think themselves accursed they were not here,

And hold their manhoods cheap whiles any speaks

That fought with us upon Saint Crispin's day.

This outlook started to be questioned during the Enlightenment, by thinkers like David Hume, Voltaire and JS Mill. However, it was probably the First World War (1914-1918) that caused the biggest change in attitudes to war. The war poet Wilfred Owen repeated Horace's line in his famous poem Dulce et Decorum Est, but this time satirically, questioning whether there is anything sweet or beautiful about modern warfare. Owen describes the sight of a fellow soldier dying from a poison gas attack.

If in some smothering dreams you too could pace
Behind the wagon that we flung him in,
And watch the white eyes writhing in his face,
His hanging face, like a devil's sick of sin;
If you could hear, at every jolt, the blood
Come gargling from the froth-corrupted lungs,
Obscene as cancer, bitter as the cud
Of vile, incurable sores on innocent tongues,
My friend, you would not tell with such high zest
To children ardent for some desperate glory,
The old Lie: Dulce et decorum est
Pro patria mori.

Nonetheless, the Second World War (1939-1945) is often used as an example of a war that was moral, because it was a war to destroy Nazism, a political philosophy dedicated to racism and genocide that was eventually to kill over 6 million people.

So is war a glorious business, where a band of brothers show wonderful bravery and are remembered for all time? Or is it a monstrous tragedy, where innocent young men are corrupted and the public are fed lies?

Attitudes to war are quite mixed and can be grouped into three types:

- **WAR IS A SUPREMELY MORAL ACTIVITY** - because it tests courage and loyalty to the highest degree and it is done in the service of your monarch or country which is an extremely selfless sacrifice of your time and comfort, perhaps your life; on this view, war does not require much moral justification (though it might need justifying in other ways, such as against the criticism that it is a waste of valuable resources): we can call this position **MILITARISM.**

- **WAR IS THE ULTIMATE IMMORAL ACTIVITY** - organising violence and cruelty on a huge scale, bringing misery to everyone involved and often misleading or brutalising soldiers and civilians on your own side as much as the opposing side; on this view, no war can be justified morally: this position is generally known as **PACIFISM**.

- **WAR IS A NECESSARY EVIL** - although it involves doing immoral things (like killing people) it can be justified if it's in a good cause and opposes something much worse; on this view, each war needs to be justified separately and the reasons for going to war need to be carefully scrutinised. This is probably the majority view in Britain today: this would be a **JUDICIAL** approach to war, known as **JUST WAR THEORY**.

MILITARISM	**PACIFISM**	**JUST WAR THEORY**
War isn't evil at all	War is completely evil	War is a necessary evil
What makes war a good thing?	What makes war a bad thing?	What makes war a necessary thing?
VICTORY?	DEATH?	INJUSTICE?
COURAGE?	SUFFERING?	GENOCIDE?
HEROISM?	CRUELTY?	INVASION?
PROGRESS?	DESTRUCTION?	THREATS?

Examples could be from actual wars or even from TV, films, stories or games

THE PRIME MINISTER'S LETTER

When a new British Prime Minister comes to power, his first task is to write four identical letters to the captains of Britain's nuclear missile submarines. These letters are delivered to the submarine captains who place them, unopened, inside two safes in the submarine control rooms. The letter from the previous Prime Minister is taken out and destroyed without being opened.

This letter instructs the submarine captain in what to do if the British state is destroyed in a nuclear attack. The Prime Minister can order the captains to do one of four things:

1. Launch the submarines' nuclear missiles at the country that attacked Britain.

2. Do not launch the nuclear missiles.

3. Go to a friendly country (such as the USA or Australia) and hand the ships and the nuclear missiles over to them to use.

4. Act according to their own judgement.

No one knows what each Prime Minister orders the submarine captains to do. When a Prime Minister leaves power their letter is destroyed unread and no former Prime Minister will speak about it.

If you had to write this "Letter of Last Resort", what would your instruction be?

At the end of each section in this book, we will return to the Letter of Last Resort and consider how each ethical philosophy might influence what a Prime Minister to write in it.

Militarism

"War makes bad men worse and good men better" - Joshua
Lawrence Chamberlain, hero of the Battle of Gettysburg (1863)

WHAT IS MILITARISM?

We will call **MILITARISM** the view that, far from being a bad thing, war
is in fact a good thing and brings out good qualities in people. Militarism
was a common view in ancient times and is still a view held in some
cultures, but it is quite unpopular in modern Western societies.
Nevertheless, just because a view is unpopular that doesn't make it
wrong. What can be said in favour of Militarism?

War tests courage to the utmost and courage might be seen as the most
important moral quality. Why courage? The importance of courage is
that it is required by every other moral quality: a kind man is only kind up
to a point if he lacks courage; similarly, if you don't have courage you
cannot be truly honest, kind or generous because the slightest threat will
make you abandon your moral principles and make you cheat, bully or
steal.

War makes courage valuable in people's eyes: it identifies courageous
people and it holds them up as role models for the rest. At the same
time, cowardice is not tolerated during war and is likely to be punished.
Perhaps only during wartime do people have a genuine admiration for
the courageous and a desire to be more courageous themselves.

War tests other moral qualities too, particularly loyalty and self-sacrifice. During wartime, communities "pull together" and neighbours help each other out. With the threat of destruction hanging over them, people put their lives into perspective, become less selfish and stop tolerating destructive behaviour in their children and neighbours so crime and other antisocial behaviour goes down.

There's a widespread feeling that these qualities become less common during peacetime. Anyone who gets nostalgic for "the Blitz Spirit" or feels that a stint of National Service would do young people some good is probably influenced by Militarism.

A Militarist can argue that war makes it clear what morality really is, and why it matters, and makes us care about it. War reminds people about their real priorities, teaches people what to value and makes society healthier. In peace time, we become **DECADENT**, which means we become morally confused, selfish and weak. Crime goes up, families break up and problems like drug addiction soar.

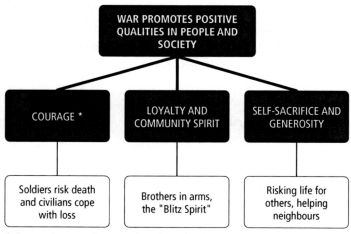

*the most important because others depend on it

ARGUING AGAINST MILITARISM

People often accuse Militarists of being "war-mongers" who try to start wars because they enjoy them. Certainly, people who believe in Militarism are much more likely to support a war, but they won't necessarily support every war. A Militarist could still object to a war on practical grounds (if war couldn't accomplish anything, or would cost too much) and many Militarists believe in an honour code that would make some wars dishonourable (for example, breaking a peace treaty). Militarists don't necessarily want to fight everybody, all the time.

It is easier to argue against Militarist claims about the beneficial effects of war. Even if courage is the most important moral quality, it's not certain that war is the only, or the best, way to foster courage. Sport can foster courage, as well as loyalty and self-sacrifice. Even during peacetime there is a need for people to do charity work, missionary work, police work - there are lots of ways for people to be courageous and for courage to be celebrated without going to war.

The other moral qualities that war is supposed to promote can also be celebrated in peace time. For example, newspapers give awards each year like "Pride of Britain Award" and "Our Hero" to ordinary people who help others, put themselves at risk or show community spirit. In 2011, toddler Rowan Rychel received a Police Award for Bravery for dialling 999 after her mother collapsed.

Even if war does encourage some very desirable qualities in people, it fosters some very undesirable ones too. Soldiers may be brave and loyal, but they can also be cruel and brutal. For example, in 2013 people were shocked by a video of a rebel soldier in Syria apparently eating an enemy's heart. The Balkan War of the 1990s had many shocking stories of soldiers using rape as a weapon of war.

During a war, communities might pull together, but they can also become suspicious and bigoted. During World War II many Italian and German families living in Britain received a lot of hostility. Some were arrested in the night, their businesses were closed down; others were attacked by mobs or deported to Canada. Over 100,000 Japanese Americans in California were rounded up and put into concentration camps by the US Government after the attack on Pearl Harbor. President Reagan apologised for this in 1988, admitting that it was based on "race prejudice and war hysteria".

Wartime propaganda can often involve lying about the enemy in order to encourage fear, indignation and hatred in people. For example, during World War 1 stories were circulated about German soldiers bayoneting babies and raping nuns to create the idea that a German soldier was a "diabolical Hun". One British general is supposed to have remarked after the war:

> "To make armies go on killing one another it is necessary to invent lies about the enemy."

This is what led US Senator Hiram Johnson (1918) to remark:

> "The first casualty in war is truth."

When you put all these criticisms of war together, the Militarist claim that war can be morally good starts to look weak. In fact, war starts to look evil. We will look later at **PACIFISM**, which claims war is completely evil, and **JUST WAR THEORY**, which claims war is sometimes a necessary evil.

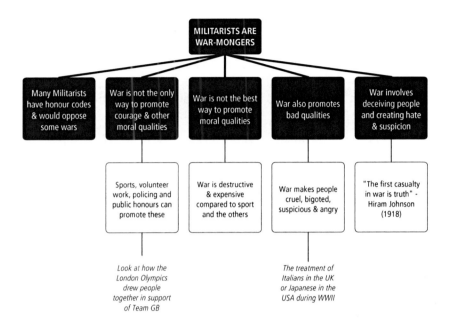

```
                        ┌─────────────────┐
                        │ MILITARISTS ARE │
                        │   WAR-MONGERS   │
                        └─────────────────┘
```

| Many Militarists have honour codes & would oppose some wars | War is not the only way to promote courage & other moral qualities | War is not the best way to promote moral qualities | War also promotes bad qualities | War involves deceiving people and creating hate & suspicion |

| | Sports, volunteer work, policing and public honours can promote these | War is destructive & expensive compared to sport and the others | War makes people cruel, bigoted, suspicious & angry | "The first casualty in war is truth" - Hiram Johnson (1918) |

Look at how the London Olympics drew people together in support of Team GB

The treatment of Italians in the UK or Japanese in the USA during WWII

HAS WAR CHANGED?

A final objection to Militarism is that it has been rendered unethical by technological and cultural change. Modern warfare involves machines that can kill on a grand scale and at a huge distance: combat like this often involves just pressing a button and you never get to see your enemy. Military drones kill targets in Afghanistan and Africa with pilots safely home in America. It's hard for a Militarist to argue that this sort of warfare makes people braver or nobler.

Then there's the availability of Weapons of Mass Destruction (**WMD**) - bacteriological (diseases), chemical (poisons) and nuclear weapons. These have the power to wipe out whole populations - perhaps the human race entirely - and might be "game-changers" that cancel out any moral value that war once had. In order for war to make people braver and nobler, there have to be some people left at the end of it but a war using WMDs might not leave any survivors.

Albert Einstein expressed this idea on several occasions with a grim joke:

> "I know not with what weapons World War 3 will be fought, but World War 4 will be fought with sticks and stones."

If WMDs mean that the next big war destroys civilisation itself, then any benefits war might have had in the past will be cancelled out.

Finally, modern Western societies are multicultural so it's likely in any war that a minority group in the population will have ethnic ties to "the enemy". One solution in the 20th C was to set up concentration camps to hold these possibly disloyal citizens; for example, the internment of 100,000 Japanese-Americans during World War 2. However, the sheer size and diversity of minority groups in a modern multicultural society makes this difficult. For example, there are now 1.3 million Japanese Americans and 3.8 million Chinese Americans, far too many for the US government to lock away without creating enormous unrest and resistance.

Even if it was possible to arrest millions of people during a war, the argument that war helps unite a community now looks weak. The majority community would only unite at the expense of certain minority communities, who would be imprisoned, deported or subjected to great oppression.

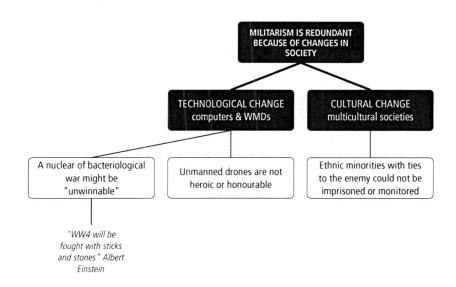

CAN WAR PRESERVE PEACE?

Militarists also make a different claim about wars, that even if they are bad in themselves they have the effect of bringing about a more stable and harmonious world. This is sometimes expressed with a Latin phrase **SI VIS PACEM PARA BELLUM** ("If you want peace, prepare for war").

This might sound contradictory, but the idea is that big military powers (like America, Russia, China, for example) are much better employed fighting small wars in different parts of the world (eg Afghanistan, Chechnya) than fighting each other. Constant small wars allow countries to "let off steam", make use of their expensive weaponry and show everyone how dangerous they are. Small wars are also watched by rival countries and they realise how risky it would be getting into a conflict, making it less likely the big powers will ever go to war. This is why lots of small wars make a catastrophic World War less likely to happen.

The idea that war preserves peace is a controversial one and can be illustrated with contrasting quotes from two American presidents:

> *"To be prepared for war is one of the most effective means of preserving peace"* - George Washington (1790)

> *"Preparation for war is a constant stimulus to suspicion and ill will"* - James Monroe (1817)

Who is right, George Washington or James Monroe? Washington thinks that being "armed and dangerous" makes a war less likely because your enemies back off. Monroe thinks this sort of behaviour makes war more likely because your enemies are suspicious of you and feel they have to frighten you off.

The idea that "the price of peace is constant small wars" is open to criticism from historians. Both of the World Wars in the 20th C had small wars leading up to them: the First World War might be said to begin with the Franco-Prussian War of 1870 and the Second World War has its origins in the Japanese invasion of Manchuria in 1931. Small wars have a tendency to **ESCALATE** into big ones.

If modern weaponry is a "game-changer" then the danger of escalation is very great indeed. If small wars escalate into a superpower conflict it might well be a nuclear conflict which will have no winners, only losers.

On the other hand, during the Cold War that lasted from 1947 to 1991, the USA and the Soviet Union never attacked each other with their nuclear weapons, despite many small wars (the Russians in Czechoslovakia and Afghanistan, the Americans in Korea and Vietnam). This suggests that maybe small wars can stop big wars from happening.

PARTISANS OF WRATH

So far we have looked at Militarists who think war produces good things in people and in society, but who share our general view about what "good things" are. War is risky to life and limb, but if you survive it makes you happier and healthier and we all value happiness and health. War threatens society with destruction and hardship, but it makes people bond together closely and this is something we can all appreciate.

David Limond (1994) considers another type of Militarist with a rather more radical philosophy. Limond calls this type a **PARTISAN OF WRATH**, inspired by a quote from the philosopher Jean-Paul Sartre (1948):

> *"Fools are always partisans of wrath."*

A Partisan of Wrath sees an intrinsic value in war itself. Regular Militarists see war as instrumentally valuable (it makes us braver, or nobler, or more selfless) but the Partisan of Wrath simply prefers waging war, whatever the outcome.

One of Limond's examples is Padraig Pearse (1879-1916), an Irish scholar and poet who took part in the 1916 Easter Uprising against British rule. Hundreds died and thousands were wounded, the leaders were executed and the Irish poet Yeats declared that a "terrible beauty is born" - which itself expresses the viewpoint of a Partisan of Wrath.

Pearse prepared for his own death in the Uprising with the 1915 essay Peace And The Gael, in which he declared:

> *"War is a terrible thing, but war is not an evil thing."*

It was Pearse's belief that God had created nations and intended them to struggle against each other, therefore when someone dies or kills in a war that expresses national pride, they are doing the will of God and praising God's creation.

> *"When war comes to Ireland, she must welcome it as she would welcome the Angel of God."*

This might sound an odd belief, but it's not uncommon for Nationalists to believe their nation is part of some divine plan and therefore dying to honour it in war is the best sort of death.

Pearse is often viewed sentimentally because he supported a war of national liberation which ultimately led to Ireland's independence. However, there are real contradictions in his view if it is held that it is the God-given duty of all nations to assert themselves through war. For one thing, it will mean fewer and fewer nations as weaker ones are annihilated or utterly subjugated. Eventually, you might suppose, there will be just one nation left that has beaten all the others, like the winner in a game of "Risk" or a gladiatorial contest. It's hard to see how God's plan could then be fulfilled, with no one for this nation to fight.

Alternatively, Pearse might be arguing that it is God's plan for the Irish nation to engage in war, but God might have different, less destructive plans for other nations (like making cheese). This then raises the question of how we can know what the divine plan for a particular nation is, and why we should trust Pearse's view that it is war, as opposed to making beautiful folk music. It is interesting that, after achieving independence, Ireland stayed neutral in World War II, suggesting that Partisans of Wrath do not always influence actual wars.

THOMAS HOBBES

The English philosopher Thomas Hobbes (1588-1679) is popular with people who support Militarism. In his 1660 book Leviathan, Hobbes argued that the original human beings lived in a **STATE OF NATURE**, with no laws or governments:

> *"The time men live without a common Power to keep them all in awe, they are in that condition which is called War; and such a war, as is of every man, against every man."*

According to Hobbes, war is the basic or natural state for human beings, with every man against every man and people only keeping their property, freedom or life by power and threat. This sort of existence is "solitary, poor, nasty, brutish and short".

Hobbes thinks people create governments and laws to escape from this State of Nature. By agreeing to obey laws we lose some of our freedom to do as we please, but we benefit from being able to trust our neighbours, engage in trade and generally not worry about being murdered or robbed at every turn. However, Hobbes warns we are always in danger of falling back into the State of Nature again through our own selfishness and violence.

If you take this view of human nature, then war is inevitable and will never be abolished, permanent peace is a fantasy and the sensible (and moral) course of action is to defend yourself with force and use aggression to put other people off attacking you. This leads to a **REALIST** view of war, which is considered next.

Hobbes was very influential, but his view of human nature is very pessimistic. Stephen Pinker (2011) argues that Hobbes is part of a

TRAGIC VISION of human nature that views us all as doomed to be irrational and destructive if left to ourselves.

Most people would agree that humans are often selfish and violent, but Hobbes seems to be ignoring our tendency to be generous and kind. Along with our urge to fight, we seem to have an urge to build communities and live peacefully. Some believe this constructive urge is actually stronger than our destructive impulse. This is what Aristotle means when he says "man is a political animal" and Stephen Pinker calls this the **UTOPIAN VISION**. According to this view, Hobbes is wrong and the real reasons for war aren't in human nature, but in the unjust and unstable societies we create. If we could solve our political problems, produce better governments and fairer societies, nobody would need war.

It's difficult to choose between the Tragic Vision and the Utopian Vision, although people are strongly influenced by their own experiences and perhaps even by their personalities. Most people are somewhere in the middle, viewing the world as a dangerous place of conflict and competition (the way Hobbes saw it) but also believing there can be progress and idealism from time to time.

REALISM

Militarism sounds very old-fashioned to many people. Words like "glory", "honour" and "heroism" aren't part of everyday language any more, at least not for most philosophers. Instead of Militarism, many modern philosophers support a different, but similar, position called **REALISM**.

Realism agrees with the viewpoint of Hobbes and the Tragic Vision that human beings are essentially selfish and destructive and therefore conflict and violence will always exist. However, Realists don't necessarily think there is anything good or noble about war. The important thing for Realists is that there isn't anything bad or immoral about it either. War is morally neutral. Sometimes it is necessary in which case there is no need for guilt or moral criticism about "doing whatever it takes" to win.

Realists like to point that war goes on between states and that states are not persons. The moral rules that apply to persons do not apply to states. States exist in a sort of rule-less world, where there are no policemen or judges to settle their disagreements or restrain them. You might say that there are international courts and international laws, but Realists reply that these institutions are created by states and enforced by states, so they only really boil down to one set of states trying to tell other states how to behave. If the international courts and laws aren't backed up by military power, then there's nothing to make other states obey them.

Realists think states are always in the middle of Hobbes' "state of war". The state of war might be polite and diplomatic, with struggles going on in embassies and trade summits, or it might be hostile and violent, with threats and attacks. But every state is trying to get the best for itself and its own people. This is what Carl von Clausewitz (1832) meant when he said "War is a continuation of foreign policy by other means."

States will try to get what they want peacefully and they will use all sorts of pressures to get their way but if peaceful means don't work then war (or the threat of war) is the only other option.

If the world really is a dog-eat-dog place, as Realists say it is, then it's actually morally wrong for a state to hold itself back with moral restrictions. By trying to behave morally, rather than putting safety and prosperity first, states are doing the wrong thing. Firstly, they are putting their own populations at risk, because moral restrictions will weaken them in conflicts with other states who aren't concerned with morality. Realists agree with the phrase "Nice guys finish last."

Secondly, by acting morally states are acting unpredictably. Imagine playing chess with someone who won't use their Queen in certain ways, because they don't think it is right to put a lady in danger. It would be very difficult to plan ahead with an opponent like that, because they wouldn't respond to normal chess moves in expected ways. This would make for a frustrating game of chess, but in international relations it makes it more likely one state will misread another's intentions and actually start a war. But if everyone agrees to act amorally and selfishly, then we all know where we stand.

Arguing against realism

Realism is difficult to argue against because it doesn't even claim to be a moral position. It's an **AMORAL** position (without any moral values).

One objection to Realism is that it is monstrous. Realists seem to be quite unconcerned by war, viewing war as simply "something that states do". Militarists think that war makes us better people and tend to believe in honourable conduct and "rules of war", but Realists don't even believe in that. You could argue that any philosophy that is happy to approve of massacres, atrocities and death on a grand scale is a monstrous philosophy that no civilised human being should agree to.

However, Realists aren't monsters. They might approve of "rules of war" and sticking to codes of conduct like the **GENEVA CONVENTION** discussed on page 110. They might agree that war should try to avoid targeting civilians, mistreating prisoners or using Weapons of Mass Destruction (**WMD**s). But Realists will do this for selfish reasons rather than moral reasons. After all, if everyone agrees to avoid using nuclear bombs or torturing prisoners, then your own cities won't be bombed and your own prisoners won't be tortured. Similarly, if you respect treaties and truces and accept surrenders, it's more likely that other countries will respect their treaties and truces with you and accept your surrender, if you later need to do it.

A more effective argument is that Realism misunderstands what a state is. A state is a community of people, with values and morals. A state that behave amorally and only ever aims to survive and get ahead will lose the approval of its own population. For example, when the USA started fighting the Vietnam War, colour television pictures of death and bombings started turning public opinion against the war. Young people burned their draft cards rather than join the Army and there were protests in colleges and in cities. President Nixon claimed in 1969:

> "North Vietnam cannot defeat or humiliate the United States.
> Only Americans can do that."

War reporter Robert Elegant (1981) famously summed up the Vietnam War, saying that:

> "... the outcome was determined not on the battlefield but on the television screen."

This suggests Realists are missing out on something and there is a moral dimension as well as a political side to conflict between states.

DEONTOLOGY AND MILITARISM

Militarism is quite strongly linked with a Deontological view of ethics, because Militarists think you have a duty to fight for your country and die for your country if you are called upon to do so. Sometimes this is expressed in the form of an exchange or **COVENANT**. Your country has given you many wonderful things in your life, such as a place to grow up, an education, a job. It might have given you wonderful experiences, like beautiful countryside, ancient traditions and art and literature. Furthermore, your country has protected you while you were growing up, with policemen close to home and soldiers on the borders. One of the moral rules that almost everyone agrees with is "Pay Your Debts" so, when a war breaks out, fighting for your country is the best way of repaying the debt you owe.

Critics of Militarism might reply that they don't owe their country this sort of debt, because they didn't choose where they were born. The countryside, culture and education might be something they didn't choose and didn't want and they might not feel any debt to pay back something they didn't ask for. Even people who do feel a debt might argue that there are better ways of repaying it than dying in battle. In fact, stopping your country going to war might be a better way of paying that debt than fighting in the war.

A key Deontological thinker is Immanuel Kant who argues that all moral rules boil down to the **CATEGORICAL IMPERATIVE**, which means acting according to universal principles. Is Militarism based on universal principles? Kant's method is to explore whether a moral rule leads to contradictions in the law of nature or contradictions in the will.

If it is right to go to war with other states, universalisability means it must be right for them to go to war with you. Militarists accept this. In fact, the idea that all countries exist in a State of Nature with regard to each other is a key idea of Thomas Hobbes and underlies the way Realists think about war. There's certainly no contradiction in nature with the idea that you can use force against force or go to war with someone who's prepared to go to war with you.

Contradictions in the will are a bigger problem. Kant asks whether you would want to live in a world where Militarist values were universal, whether it would be something a rational person could wish for. Many Realists would say we really do live in such a grim, competitive world, but there's also evidence to suggest we don't and that states sometimes act morally rather than selfishly.

As a student of philosophy, you will need to study the evidence and decide for yourself whether you really do, or really want to, live in a world where war is acceptable, admirable and inevitable.

You should consider whether modern weaponry is a "game-changer". If modern warfare is so destructive that no one could win a modern war, then there is a contradiction of the will involved in trying to universalise Militarism.

AGAPE AND MILITARISM

AGAPE, or selfless love, would seem to be quite opposed to Militarism. After all, what could be more opposed to loving someone than trying to kill them and challenging them to try to kill you?

However, you should remember that agape is not the same as liking someone. Agape is a detached sort of love that means caring for someone's overall wellbeing and wishing the best for them. It doesn't mean having "warm fuzzy feelings". A dentist can act on Agape while drilling your teeth and a surgeon can act on Agape while carrying out an operation that leads to someone's death. More to the point, an executioner could act on Agape while executing someone. In the Middle Ages it used to be a tradition for an executioner to ask his victim's forgiveness and people like Anne Boleyn and Mary Queen of Scots forgave their executioners before being beheaded. The forgiveness was meant show there was no personal ill-will involved.

So can a soldier act on Agape while killing another soldier? In the 4th C St Ambrose and his student St Augustine of Hippo both considered this. They decided that using force to defend yourself was selfish, but Agape demands that you do everything in your power to protect or rescue an innocent person, even if that means using force. So fighting to save others is loving and good and, extending this logically, Agape would not oppose someone fighting to defend their country. This idea led Augustine to develop **JUST WAR THEORY**, which is considered later.

There's still a big gulf between Agape and Militarism. The Militarist sees war as a good thing, but for Ambrose and Augustine there is always something tragic about war. Augustine recommends that soldiers should feel intense guilt about the killing they do. During the Middle Ages, if a soldier killed someone in a war they were supposed to do a year of penance (fasting and prayer). It's not clear how seriously people actually took this, but the point is that Agapeic ethics will always view war as an evil, at best a necessary evil and not a good. This is why someone who bases their ethics on love will never be entirely comfortable with Militarism.

As a student of philosophy, you'll need to decide for yourself whether it's psychologically possible to love someone while attempting to kill them or destroy their home.

TELEOLOGY AND MILITARISM

There might be some small common ground between Agape and Militarism, but **TELEOLOGICAL** (Consequentialist) ethics are almost completely opposed to Militarism.

A Militarist regards war as a good thing because it is supposed to lead to various good consequences - people being brave, noble, self-sacrificing, for example. A Consequentialist will also focus on the consequences of war, but won't select only the good ones. Consequentialism involves looking at all the consequences of war, including the bad ones. So for every soldier who is brave and loyal another one is cowardly and cruel. These cancel each other out. On top of this, the huge amount of killing and destruction that goes on in war needs to be added in to the calculations. It's not at all clear how many dead soldiers cancel out the value of one heroic soldier, but since 16 million people died in World War 1 and over 60 million died in World War 2 it seems fair to say that no amount of personal heroism is ever really going to make up for that.

Militarists also tend to focus on the benefits of war for their own people, but Consequentialists will look at the consequences for everyone, including the enemy. For example, in the 1990-1991 Gulf War, the Coalition forces suffered 378 casualties, far less than some people feared. However, Iraqi casualties were in the tens of thousands. Overall, the consequences of the war were immensely destructive.

The key difference between Teleology and Militarism comes down to this: Consequentialists believe that the consequences alone determine whether something is right or wrong; Militarists think there's something good about war itself, even if the consequences are terrible.

Consequentialism and Realism are much more closely linked. Realists don't claim there's anything good about war; they just argue that it's a means to an end. If the end is good, then war is a justifiable means. This is exactly the way Consequentialists tend to think about things. But what are the "good ends" that can justify a war? Most Realists argue that states aim to increase their power, security and prosperity. This means, if a war makes your country stronger, safer and richer, it's a good war.

Modern wars are so expensive few countries end up richer at the end of a war and the loss of life means few countries are stronger either. War might make a country safer if it removes a threat, but it might make a country less safe if it creates more enemies. This is why Realists and Consequentialists are rarely in favour of wars.

Consequentialists don't agree about what consequences make something good. John Stuart Mill (1863) argued that good consequences involve making people happy. Now very few wars tend to increase happiness so if you value happiness more than power and safety you will probably reject Realism. Peter Singer (1979) argues that good consequences involve satisfying people's preferences. This seems to fit better with Realism, since there are times when people very clearly prefer war. However, Singer (1975) argues that animals' preferences count as well as humans' preferences. The destructive impact on the environment of modern warfare surely means that wars produce more bad consequences than good.

As a student of philosophy, you will need to decide for yourself what good consequences are and then decide whether a war ever produces more good consequences than bad ones.

ARETE AND MILITARISM

Consequentialism doesn't sit well with Militarism, but Militarism and Areteic ethics are made for each other. Areteic ethics, or Virtue Ethics, focus on what makes a person into a virtuous human being and what produces a society with what Aristotle calls **EUDAIMONIA**. Eudaimonia is sometimes translated as "happiness" but it means a sort of general flourishing; a fulfilling of potential. You can have Eudaimonia in your life even while you are suffering great setbacks. For example, while Londoners were being bombed during the Blitz in 1940-1941, there was (we are told) a huge upsurge in community spirit as neighbours reached out to neighbours and people responded bravely and generously to those who had lost their homes and their families. This is Eudaimonia.

Militarists claim that war actually promotes Eudaimonia, but peace can destroy it. They might argue that, in peace time, neighbours don't even know each other, fear of crime causes people to fortify their homes and the community spirit fades away.

Eudaimonia is something a person can try to create within themselves, by practising the virtues. The Cardinal Virtues are **FORTITUDE** (courage), **PRUDENCE** (practical wisdom or thoughtfulness), **TEMPERANCE** (self control) and **JUSTICE**. War provides people with the chance to practise and improve their Virtues, especially courage. When you find the perfect balance of Virtues in your life (which Aristotle calls the "Golden Mean") you will enjoy Eudaimonia, even if you are in daily danger of being killed.

Militarists sometimes back their claims up by pointing out that war experiences produce particularly fine leaders, like Winston Churchill. Leaders whose characters were shaped by war might also be the best in peace-time. For example, Britain's post-war leaders created the Welfare

State and the NHS. The last British Prime Minister who fought in World War II was James Callaghan (1976-9).

American journalist Tom Brokaw (1998) calls the people who grew up in the Depression and fought in World War II "the Greatest Generation". The endured a lot of hardship, fought Nazism because it was "the right thing to do" and when the war was over they built America into a superpower.

> *"It is, I believe, the greatest generation any society has ever produced."*

In other words, these people and the society they created possessed Eudaimonia because they had values of "personal responsibility, duty, honour and faith".

There's a sentimental appeal to these arguments, but are they true? Not everybody becomes a wonderful person through fighting in a war; Hitler fought in the First World War and it didn't seem to improve him. Not every society acquires Eudaimonia through hardship; German society suffered great hardship in the 1920s and 1930s and it produced Nazism. Ideas like the "Blitz Spirit" and the "Greatest Generation" might be myths. During the Blitz there was also crime and looting and a rise in Anti-Semitism. Over in America the "Greatest Generation" had strongly racist and sexist views and started a nuclear arms race with the Soviet Union called the Cold War.

However, other philosophers are prepared to be less sentimental. Friedrich Nietzsche argued that all self-aware creatures are driven by a **WILL TO POWER**. The Will to Power drives us to discipline ourselves and dominate others and we are most fully and uniquely ourselves when we are doing this. Nietzsche wasn't thinking specifically of war when he suggested this, but his ideas fit with Militarism pretty well. They also support the idea that we develop some sort of Virtue or Arete through conflict.

Nietzsche's ideas were seized upon by the very people the Greatest Generation went out to fight - the Fascists, especially the Italian dictator Benito Mussolini.

> *"[Fascism] wants man to be active and to engage in action with all his energies ... Life [is] a struggle in which it behoves a man to win for himself a really worthy place." (The Doctrines of Fascism, 1935)*

This of course is the problem with Arete as an ethic of war. It's just as popular with Fascists and Nazis who have their own idea of what "Eudaimonia" means. These people are in fact what David Limond (1994) calls **PARTISANS OF WRATH** and for them Eudaimonia actually means being at war.

As a student of philosophy, you will need to decide for yourself whether war and hardship improve people or not and whether Eudaimonia is a coherent concept that a society should aim for, or fight a war for.

CHRISTIANITY AND MILITARISM

Most people don't think of Jesus in a military context, but Christian Militarists claim that Jesus would support their values.

Firstly, there are Bible passages where Jesus seems to approve of violence:

> "I come not to bring peace, but to bring a sword." (Matthew 10: 34)

> "If you don't have a sword, sell your cloak and buy one." (Luke 22: 36)

Secondly, there is one famous biblical event where Jesus is violent:

> "[Jesus] made a whip out of cords, and drove all from the temple area, both sheep and cattle; he scattered the coins of the money changers and overturned their tables." (John 2: 15)

Other details suggest Jesus might have approved of war. Jesus praises the faith of one Roman Centurion, but never criticises his job (Matthew 8: 5-13) and other Centurions are presented in the Bible as true believers, for example, the first non-Jew to convert to Christianity is a Roman Centurion (Acts 10: 22-35). When Jesus is arrested, one of his Disciples pulls out a sword. Another of Jesus' Disciples is known as Simon the Zealot - and the Zealots were a sect of violent anti-Roman terrorists.

Christian Militarists will argue from this that there is no conflict between Christianity and Militarism - you can be a good Christian and a good soldier at the same time.

However, there are other interpretations. Whenever Jesus talks about a "sword" he might be using symbolism. The "sword" might mean the courage to stand up for your faith. The story where Jesus overturns the moneychangers' tables (John 2:15; Matthew 21:12) never actually mentions Jesus hurting anyone, just disrupting their business; the whip seems to be to drive out the animals being bought and sold in the Temple. It's possible that, as soon as they converted to Christianity, the Roman Centurions all quit their jobs - something the Bible writers perhaps thought was so obvious it didn't need to be said. Simon the Zealot could have been a reformed Zealot, one who had given up violence to follow Jesus.

More to the point, only a very small number of Jesus' sayings and actions could be taken to support war. However, a huge number support loving your enemies, forgiving your enemies, turning the other cheek and showing love to people who want to hurt you. The Militarist passages are not typical of Jesus' teachings.

If you are studying philosophy from a Christian perspective, you will need to decide for yourself whether the idea of a "Christian Militarist" makes sense and whether these biblical stories and sayings support it.

THE MILITARIST'S LETTER OF LAST RESORT

If the British Prime Minister were a Militarist, what instruction would they put in the Letter of Last Resort?

You might think they would simply order the captains to fire their missiles in retaliation, but this isn't obviously true.

Militarists see a positive value in war, but a war that destroys human civilisation (or even the human species) can't benefit anybody. If a Militarist is inspired by Consequentialism or Arete they might be reluctant to order the missiles to be fired.

In fact, if a Militarist Prime Minister thinks this way, they would probably instruct the captains to hand their ships over to a friendly power. This way, some of the traditions and values of the Royal Navy (which a Militarist would think are a positive thing in this world) would continue to thrive.

However, some Militarists might disagree, if they feel they have a moral duty to achieve vengeance. This is a Deontological argument that we have a moral duty to our dead families, friends and fellow countrymen to punish their attackers. According to this view, it would be immoral NOT to fire the missiles in retaliation.

Revenge is a complicated moral idea. Christian ethics rejects revenge, arguing instead that we should "turn the other cheek" when we are struck. In Christian thought, revenge is not the same as justice, because justice is mixed with mercy. Therefore revenge is always a temptation, never a moral duty.

Immanuel Kant would come to the same conclusion for a different reason. If the idea of pursuing revenge were universalised, we would have a world where nobody ever forgave anything and feuds would make ordinary life impossible. This is what Kant calls a **CONTRADICTION IN THE WILL**, because you want to protect your loved ones by threatening anyone who hurts them, but by universalising this you have a world where your loved ones are in even more danger than before.

What about a Prime Minister who is a Realist? A Realist will not be concerned with the moral rights or wrongs of retaliating, only with whether it accomplishes anything. Clearly, if Britain has been destroyed then the nuclear deterrent has failed. Firing the missiles now won't achieve anything.

The irony of the Realist's position is that the nuclear deterrent only works so long as enemy countries believe you have instructed the captains to fire the missiles. It is their belief that makes the deterrent work. This is why the contents of the Letters of Last Resort are never known. If it was revealed that Prime Ministers in the past had told the captains not to retaliate, then an enemy country might be tempted to gamble that the current Prime Minister has also given this advice. This makes a nuclear attack more likely.

A Realist Prime Minister is in the strange position of either instructing the captains to retaliate even though it is futile and pointless, or telling them not to retaliate but keeping this a secret, a sort of huge doomsday bluff. This also means that Britain would be paying for a multi-billion pound weapon system that is never going to be used. A Realist might believe such a hugely expensive deception keeps the country safe, but other ethicists will view it rather differently.

KEY TERMS

- **EUDAIMONIA**
- **FORTITUDE**
- **MILITARISM**
- **PARTISAN OF WRATH**
- **REALISM**
- **STATE OF NATURE**
- **TRAGIC VISION**
- **UTOPIAN VISION**

FURTHER READING

- **DOWER, N** - The Ethics of War & Peace (2009), Polity, Ch 2
- **FIALA, A** - Practical Pacifism (2008), Algora, Ch 2
- **HOBBES, T** - Leviathan (1660, 2008), Oxford, Ch 13
- **OREND, B** - The Morality of War (2006), Broadview, Ch 8
- **PINKER, S** - The Better Angels of Our Nature, Penguin, Ch 2
- **WALZER, M** - Just & Unjust Wars (1977), Basic Books, Ch 1

SELF-ASSESSMENT QUESTIONS

1. Explain what is good about war.

2. Outline the strengths and weaknesses of Militarism as an ethical philosophy.

3. What would be a Militarist interpretation of a conflict in the world today?

4. Analyse the Militarist beliefs contained in a comic, TV show, video game, film or song.

5. Is Militarism out of date? Does it matter?

6. Does the philosophy of a Partisan of Wrath involve a Contradiction in Nature or a Contradiction in the Will or both? Or neither?

7. To what extent is the Bible a Partisan of Wrath?

8. Does history support a Tragic (Hobbesian) or Utopian Vision of human nature?

9. Is there a moral problem with a Realist approach to war?

10. Can a Christian be a Realist about war? What features of the Bible or Christian theology can be used in support of this?

Pacifism

"Does it never strike you as puzzling that it is wicked to kill one person, but glorious to kill ten thousand?" Lewis Richardson, *Statistics of Deadly Quarrels (1950:130)*

WHAT IS PACIFISM?

The **PACIFIST** position, the opposite of the Militarist one, is that war is a great evil, perhaps the greatest of evils, and the moral course of action is always to resist the temptation to go to war. In the past people who held this opinion were often taunted with cowardice or subjected to persecution, but it is an increasingly popular view in modern Western society, just as the Militarist view declines in popularity.

Some people use "pacifism" to mean rejecting violence generally. There are some individuals who genuinely do reject all violence as unethical, even to the point of refusing to defend themselves. In Asian religions this sort of complete harmlessness is known as **AHIMSA** and a religion which practises this is Jainism.

However, we are using Pacifism in a rather more specific sense to mean the idea that war, rather than just violence, is evil. A Pacifist is anti-war and may or may not be anti-violence as well.

What is ethically special about war that makes it different from ordinary violence? For one thing, there is the destructiveness of war. In day-to-day violence people might get a black eye or a broken bone; in extreme cases they might die but this is often unintended. In war, killing is the precise intention and every effort is made to kill as quickly and effectively as possible.

The other feature of war is the scale of the destruction. Day-to-day violence affects individuals, but war is directed at whole armies, even whole populations. This destructiveness isn't just limited to people, but buildings, wildlife, the whole environment will be destroyed. In the past, wars involved burning fields and sacking towns but modern weapons of war can make huge areas uninhabitable.

A final feature of war is its political purpose. Day-to-day violence is usually motivated by anger or a personal grievance (such as revenge), occasionally by greed or malice (such as an armed robbery). This doesn't excuse violence, but it makes violence something that people can sometimes justify or else come to feel guilty about later. War is killing in the name of politics, which means killing people who are not your personal enemies. The soldier in war stands to gain nothing personally by killing and has no personal reason to wish his victim dead. He is "following orders" and treating the human beings he is killing as "targets" or "hostiles". There is no need to feel guilty. This cold and callous quality in war is something that disgusts many Pacifists.

CONSCIENTIOUS OBJECTORS

A common response for Pacifists is to refuse to fight in a war. Pacifists insist that their refusal to fight isn't based on cowardice or disloyalty, but on their consciences. This is why since the First World War they have adopted the title of **CONSCIENTIOUS OBJECTORS**.

In the First World War about 7,000 Pacifists refused to fight but were willing to help the country by working in non-combat roles such as medical orderlies, stretcher-bearers, ambulance drivers, cooks or labourers. Other Pacifists, known as Absolute Conscientious Objectors, rejected any involvement in the war. By the end of the war, 8,608 Conscientious Objectors had been arrested and judged by military tribunals. Over 4,500 went sent to do work of national importance such as farming. However, 528 were sentenced to imprisonment, including the philosopher Bertrand Russell, who spent a year in solitary confinement. Conditions were made very hard for the Conscientious Objectors and 69 of them died in prison.

During the Second World War a more tolerant approach was taken. A total of 59,192 people in Britain registered as Conscientious Objectors (**CO**s). However, as the war dragged on public opinion turned against COs or "conchies". Over 70 city councils dismissed COs who were working for them. Some employees refused to work alongside COs. Some employers sacked all those claiming to be Pacifists.

In 1948 the United Nations Declaration of Human Rights was written with this passage included:

> *"Everyone has the right to freedom of thought, conscience and religion."*

The right to conscience is commonly understood to include the right to refuse to kill.

During the Vietnam War the United States had to introduce conscription and over 9,000 men were prosecuted for refusing to be drafted into the US Army. Some young men burnt their draft cards in public while others left the country rather than serve in the war. While some of them might have had other motives (self preservation, a Realist view that the war was pointless, a Just War view that the war was unjust), some of them were certainly ethical Pacifists.

Some Conscientious Objectors refuse to fight, but agree to do other non-combatant work to help their country during a war. Others COs go further than this, refusing to do any work that might help the war effort. Many pacifists have bravely choosing punishment, and even execution, rather than go to war or help with a war.

Recently, some Pacifists have argued that it is right, not just to refuse to fight, but to refuse to pay taxes to the Government that would go towards supporting a war they disagree with. This was stated by the Christian writer and peace campaigner Leo Tolstoy (1910):

> "If only ... each private individual understood that the payment of taxes wherewith to hire and equip soldiers, and, above all, army-service itself, are not matters of indifference, but are bad and shameful actions by which he not only permits but participates in murder."

Others object to taking part in Remembrance Services to honour the dead of the World Wars. They argue that, although the soldiers died bravely, the orders they were following were wrong; moreover, these celebrations can be accused of glorifying warfare and supporting a Militarist philosophy. Supporters of the Peace Pledge Union choose to wear a white poppy in place of the traditional red poppy.

What about the Nazis?

It's a fair question to ask Pacifists what they would do if faced with a foreign government that uses a country's armed forces to invade its neighbours, carry out massacres and genocides and spread an ideology of hate and inequality. In other words, what would they do if faced with Nazis?

We'll answer that question by looking at different types of Pacifism in turn.

DEFENCISM

DEFENCISM (or defensivism) is perhaps the weakest form of Pacifism. This is the belief that war is morally acceptable only as a form of self-defence against someone attacking your own country. War for any reason other than self-defence is unethical.

This is a popular idea and it's common to hear people criticise their country getting involved in foreign conflicts by saying "What right do we have getting involved?" Following this line of thought, a country should maintain a small army to defend its borders or coasts, but not a large army to fight in other parts of the world.

There are practical difficulties with this. Many countries believe that "self-defence" has to start by dealing with threats to national security far away, rather than waiting until an enemy army is at their border. For example, the invasion of Iraq in was justified as self-defence, because it was claimed the Iraqi regime had Weapons of Mass Destruction that could be used against Britain. Prime Minister Tony Blair commented:

> *"So far as our objective, it is disarmament, not régime change - that is our objective. Now I happen to believe the regime of Saddam is a very brutal and repressive regime, I think it does enormous damage to the Iraqi people ... so I have got no doubt Saddam is very bad for Iraq, but on the other hand I have got no doubt either that the purpose of our challenge from the United Nations is disarmament of weapons of mass destruction, it is not regime change." (Interview 29.10.2011)*

The other practical problem is that defending your borders is not usually enough for a country to feel secure. For example, the 2006 Lebanon War happened because Hezbollah groups in Lebanon were firing missiles over the border into Israel, and the 2009 invasion of Palestine by Israel was justified for the same reason: random rocket attacks had occurred for several months beforehand. Israel also occupies the Golan Heights, which were part of Syria, for fear of the same thing. Self-defence can be a motivation to invade other countries, which most Pacifists (and many Just War Theorists) would object to.

Self-defence can also justify tactics that are usually considered unethical, such as the policy of **RENDITION** whereby suspects are kidnapped and removed to countries which sanction torture. Instead of having an army to defend it, a country could just acquire nuclear missiles and threaten to use them against anyone threatening its borders. This might be effective but most Realists would reject it (because it leads to nuclear escalation) as would Just War Theorists (because it's disproportionate to what the enemy might have done).

Since Defencists approve of war and killing in self-defence, so it's difficult to see why they object to it in other situations. A Realist might argue for defensive strategies because getting involved in foreign wars is risky and expensive, but a Defencist is saying that it's morally acceptable to fight a war against people who invade you, but morally wrong to fight against people who invade your neighbour or massacre their own civilians or protect international terrorists. This doesn't seem consistent, but as soon as you allow war to be fought for these other reasons you're no longer a Pacifist at all.

What about the Nazis?

Defencists have to argue that Nazism is none of their business, so long as their own borders are safe. In World War 2, a Defencist Britain would not have declared war on the Nazis unless the Nazis first tried to attack Britain. Even if that happened, a Defencist Britain would not have invaded Occupied Europe to defeat Nazism. The invasions of Poland, France, Russia and many other countries would have made no difference to this and neither would the Holocaust.

As a student of philosophy, you'll have to decide for yourself whether this would have been an ethically satisfactory position to take.

PACIFICISM

Pacificism is defined by Martin Caedel (1987) as wishing to promote peace, but being prepared to use war to do it. A Pacificist might be prepared to back military interventions which promote the goal of global peace. The US government claimed its "War On Terror" and the invasion of Afghanistan to destroy Al-Qaeda was in the cause of global peace, which would make this a Pacificist war.

Pacificism is clearly more like regular Pacifism than stay-at-home Defencism. A Pacificist might even argue that a country should surrender rather than fight against an invader, because it might be easier to bring about peace through protest, non-violent resistance and diplomacy. Pacificists will argue that wars are immoral if they don't lead to peace and very few wars do increase peace, so a Pacificist might, in practice, act just like a normal Pacifist. However, Pacificism is also flexible because it is pro-peace rather than anti-war. A Pacificist might approve of a war to remove a bloodthirsty tyrant who was slaughtering his own people or disarm a rogue state that was threatening its neighbours.

Pacificism seems to be the philosophy many countries act on, since they often claim they are fighting wars to create a more peaceful world. This is part of the problem with Pacificism. The Roman Empire created a peaceful environment, called the **PAX ROMANA** ("Roman Peace"). For about a century the British Empire imposed the "Pax Britannica" on the countries and oceans it ruled. Pacificism seems to approve of imperialism, which is when powerful empires complete dominate smaller countries and govern their affairs. Many people value peace, but they also value freedom. However, a Pacificist is committed to supporting a powerful country's invasions if they bring about a lasting peace, even if it's a peace based on force.

Not everyone agrees that imperialism is the best way to bring about peace. Empires tend to collapse sooner or later, often with great violence. The Balkan Wars of 1991-1999 killed 140,000 people and are seen by many historians as resulting from the collapse of the empire of the Soviet Union. In the 21st C trade and commerce seems to be the best way of making sure countries have more to gain from being peaceful than from fighting.

However, even if countries can live together peacefully without a big empire dominating them, there is a practical problem for Pacificists. It's difficult to know what the consequences of war will be, even if you know who will win it. For example, the US-led invasion of Iraq in 2003 led to a long period of bloodshed and turmoil for that country and perhaps contributed to international terrorism in other countries and not the peace many hoped for at the time.

What about the Nazis?

A Pacificist Britain might well have gone to war with the Nazis exactly as happened in 1939. In fact, Pacificists might have urged Britain to wage war on Nazism even earlier, such as when Hitler first came to power in 1933.

This shows another issue with Pacificism, which is that in some situations Pacificists will be even quicker to start a war than Militarists. As a student of philosophy, you will have to decide whether Pacificism helps solve problems or only creates more.

SELECTIVE PACIFISM

Selective or **CONTINGENT** Pacifists believe that war is evil only as a matter of degree and they only oppose wars involving weapons or tactics they consider unethical.

Exactly which weapons and tactics are unethical is difficult to agree on. In the Middle Ages the authorities were appalled by the devastating power of the crossbow and the Church tried to ban it from being used. There are Militarists who believe in an honour code which forbids them from breaking an alliance or making a surprise attack, which is a form of Selective Pacifism.

The most common type of Selective Pacifism today objects to using Weapons of Mass Destruction (WMDs). These are nuclear or chemical and biological weapons. These weapons have uniquely devastating power (which makes them intrinsically wrong), and a war that uses such weapons is not "winnable" (so their use is instrumentally wrong).

This view was set out in the famous **RUSSELL-EINSTEIN MANIFESTO**, published in 1955 by the philosopher Bertrand Russell, the scientist Albert Einstein and other prominent thinkers. The Manifesto called for world leaders to abandon the use of nuclear weapons:

> "In view of the fact that in any future world war nuclear weapons will certainly be employed, and that such weapons threaten the continued existence of mankind, we urge the governments of the world to realise, and to acknowledge publicly, that their purpose cannot be furthered by a world war, and we urge them, consequently, to find peaceful means for the settlement of all matters of dispute between them."

There are some Realists who might come to the same conclusion about WMDs being instrumentally wrong and since the Manifesto no country has used nuclear weapons. This should alert you to a problem with Selective Pacifism - it's hardly Pacifism at all if Militarists and Realists believe the same thing.

Selective Pacifism can also be criticised for making distinctions between different types of warfare that don't stand up to closer inspection. For example, the atomic bomb dropped on the Japanese city of Hiroshima in 1945 killed 70,000-80,000 people. The earlier firebombing of Tokyo by the US Air Force used conventional explosives and killed 100,000 people. The RAF Bomber Command killed similar numbers in its 1945 raids on Hamburg and Dresden using conventional explosives.

Most Pacifists seem to object to the mass killing in war, but Selective Pacifists seem to be saying that some mass killing is morally acceptable but other mass killing isn't, it depends how the killing is done. Many people regard this as an unimportant distinction.

Selective Pacifism can also be criticised for making wars worse. If a war must be fought, then the moral thing is to win it quickly with few casualties. Selective Pacifists instead approve of wars that last longer, with more casualties, so long as proscribed WMDs are not used. An example of this is discussed below.

However, despite these criticisms Selective Pacifism can be seen to work. Since the Second World War, countries have agreed never again to use nuclear weapons. Several countries own them (for example, USA, Britain, France, Russia, China) but they never have been used since in war. Even when nuclear-armed countries have been involved in war, they have chosen to use only conventional weapons. This would seem to be a victory for Selective Pacifism.

What about the Nazis?

The bombing raids on Dresden are still a controversial event in the Second World War. Bomber Command believed these raids shortened the war by weakening the Nazi war machine. They forced the Nazis to divert resources (money, weapons, manpower) to defending German cities rather than fighting Allied troops in Europe. Selective Pacifists argue that Dresden was a civilian target (and was crowded with refugees as well) that served no strategic purpose - it was a medieval city renowned for its artists.

There are people today who continue to argue that the bombing of Dresden was a war crime, but others argue just as forcefully that the bombing was necessary to shorten the war. As a student of philosophy, you will need to decide whether Selective Pacifism is helpful for deciding how war should be fought.

ABSOLUTE PACIFISM

Absolute Pacifism is the belief that it is never right to take part in war, even in self-defence. Many Absolute Pacifists think that the value of human life is so high that nothing can justify killing a person deliberately. This is not an easy principle to live up to. For example, it would be wrong to use violence to rescue an innocent person who is being attacked and may be killed - this is not a comfortable moral position for most people. This is one reason why most Pacifists are Contingent Pacifists rather than Absolute Pacifists. Contingent Pacifists think peace is an ideal, but admit there might be circumstances which could make war acceptable, but Absolute Pacifists deny this. For them, war is **ALWAYS** wrong.

The idea of an absolute ban on war and violence is quite an extreme idea for most people, which might be why this sort of ethical thinking is usually associated with religion. In Indian religions (Jainism, Hinduism, Buddhism) this absolute rejection of violence is called ahimsa. Faced with the decision to kill or be killed, ahimsa claims it is better to be killed than to kill. It is difficult for non-religious people to accept this, as Gandhi (1928) admitted:

> *"My religion is based on truth and non-violence. Truth is my God. Non-violence is the means of realising Him."*

Absolute Pacifists like Gandhi are not completely self-destructive. They often argue that the choice between killing or being killed is a **FALSE DILEMMA**. There are usually lots of other options besides these two, if you use your imagination and take time and trouble to find them. For example, in 1948 Gandhi was able to bring violence between Indian Hindus (like himself) and Muslims to end by fasting-unto-death. He refused to eat until the two sides agreed to a peaceful resolution. It worked and when politicians agreed to back down and renounce violence Gandhi broke his fast by sipping orange juice.

Nonetheless, not every situation can be solved by peaceful means. If every other option fails and only "kill-or-be-killed" is left, the Absolute Pacifist has to be prepared to die rather than fight. This can also mean allowing your country to be invaded and your people to be oppressed or enslaved. Absolute Pacifists often argue that even this is not as bad as war. Peaceful resistance can continue even after an invasion and eventually the invaders can be brought to see that what they have done is unjust and they will stop their oppression. This might take a long time with many casualties, but it will still be better than war.

What about the Nazis?

Nazis are a real test-case for Absolute Pacifism, because here surely is a regime that would definitely not have been influenced by someone like Gandhi fasting to death. Non-violence would have meant allowing the Nazis to conquer Europe, perhaps Britain and Russia, maybe even the world. The Nazis had their own hate-filled ideology that would have given them no concerns about executing protesters and brainwashing children into rejecting Pacifism when they grew up. Meanwhile, genocide would make the cost of non-violence very high indeed.

It's difficult to believe that Nazis could have been persuaded to take a different course by Pacifists. But we will never know for sure. As a student of philosophy, you will need to decide for yourself whether Absolute Pacifism is persuasive and whether it can be successful in the world as it is.

ARGUING AGAINST PACIFISM

Pacifism is often criticised for being a "clean hands policy". This means that Pacifists are only concerned with keeping the own consciences pure while other people have to go and do the morally awful work of killing. Some times Pacifists are condemned as "free riders"; people who want to have all the benefits of living in a country but don't want to do the unpleasant and disgusting fighting that is sometimes necessary to protect their way of life. Some critics go further, saying the Pacifism is in fact an excuse for cowardice or laziness rather than being a moral position at all.

These criticisms are **AD HOMINEM** arguments. Rather than attacking Pacifism they are attacking Pacifists. They don't tackle the question of whether Pacifism is right or wrong because they are busy attacking Pacifists for being bad people. Most philosophers consider ad hominem arguments to be the weakest sort of criticism, or even no criticism at all.

If this sort of criticism deserves a reply, it should be said that Pacifists often pay a high price for their beliefs. Many suffer discrimination, some are imprisoned, some even die. To be sure, going to war is more dangerous than going to prison, but it has its compensations: the company of friends and fellow-soldiers, the respect of civilians, military honours and a wage. A Pacifist might end up losing all of these.

A different criticism of Pacifism is its unworldliness. It is widely believed that Pacifism can never be a national policy - it will only work if no one wants to attack your country or if enemy nations are also committed to Pacifism. In any other circumstances adopting a Pacifist policy will result in your country being conquered. In his acceptance speech for the Nobel Prize, Barack Obama (2009) praised Pacifists like Gandhi and Martin Luther King, but added:

"A nonviolent movement could not have halted Hitler's armies. Negotiations cannot convince Al-Qaeda's leaders to lay down their arms."

This means that at best, Pacifists can only put moral pressure on a government to pursue diplomatic solutions. But this is not a small thing. The idea of seeking non-violent solutions to disputes between nations now plays a significant part in international politics, particularly through the work of the United Nations. This might be a direct result of Pacifist principles gaining respect.

Another criticism says that, because the world is not perfect, war is not always wrong. This is the argument that Pacifism is morally deficient.

Militarists would say that states have a duty to protect their citizens and citizens have a duty to carry out certain tasks if the state finds itself at war.

Just War Theory would say that sometimes atrocities take place which are so bad that you have a moral duty to stop them which is greater than your moral duty to avoid using violence.

According to arguments like these, it doesn't matter that Pacifists are motivated by respect for human life and a love of peace: their refusal to participate in war does not make them noble idealists, but people who are failing to carry out an important moral obligation.

However, things might not be this straightforward. In the past, Britain and America took many Africans as slaves and this arrangement certainly benefited the citizens of the American South, in particular. But that didn't mean people had a moral obligation to support slavery, just because it was official government policy and benefited the citizens. In fact, the "noble idealists" won the day and slavery was abolished. People can never have an absolute obligation to obey the state, and objecting to war might be one of the occasions when they are justified in being disobedient.

This argument is saying that Pacifism has no place in the face of extreme evil. This boils down to the famous quotation often attributed to the 18th-C politician Edmund Burke (1729-1797):

> "The only thing necessary for the triumph of evil is for good men to do nothing."

The Second World War is often cited as an example of a war against clear moral wickedness. The Nazis had a stated policy of systematic cruelty, racial supremacy and genocide. Much the same could be said of Japanese imperialism in the East at the same time. In 1941, an editorial in the Times Literary Supplement read:

> "We have discovered that there is something more horrible than war - the killing of the spirit in the body, the Nazi contempt for the individual man. The world reeks with the foulness of the crimes in occupied Europe, where a Dark Age has begun anew."

Can it be moral to do nothing to prevent evil? This is a powerful dilemma for the Pacifist to grapple with. It is often said that "two wrongs do not make a right". Using violence to prevent an atrocity can end up only making the atrocity worse. This is what Gandhi meant when he said:

> "An eye for an eye only ends up making the whole world blind."

However a different, but equally moral, view is expressed by Clifford

Simmons, whose 1965 book The Objectors presents the testimony of five COs during the Second World War:

"I could not stand aside from the experiences of others … I still believed that the position of the pacifist was ultimately right but I was beginning to realise that, at the same time, I could not stand aside from the struggle which was engulfing my contemporaries." Clifford Simmons

Of course a Pacifist is not committed to "doing nothing" or "standing aside". There are many other measures that can be taken to restrain other nations besides violence: there are economic sanctions, boycotts, diplomatic agreements and bringing in neutral nations as mediators or peacekeepers. These measures were not used enough in the past and many people feel they are still not being used enough today. A powerful objection to the invasion of Iraq in 2003 was that diplomatic steps had not yet been exhausted (Egypt under President Mubarak was trying to broker an agreement that included 5,000 new weapons inspectors), and there was more work for existing UN weapons inspectors to do which could have made the war unnecessary.

As a student of philosophy, you will need to decide for yourself whether Pacifism is unworldly or merely idealistic. Is there something morally deficient in Pacifism? Is non-violence a better solution?

ELIZABETH ANSCOMBE

It would be a mistake to think that the only people criticising Pacifism are warlike Militarists and amoral Realists. An interesting criticism of Pacifism was put forward by the Irish philosopher G Elizabeth Anscombe in 1961. As a student Anscombe had opposed Britain joining the Second World War, arguing the war would be fought for unjust reasons and using unjust means. After the War, she continued to argue for a Christian ethic of war and peace. She led a protest against US President Truman being awarded an honorary degree by Oxford University because she considered him a "mass murderer" for ordering the atomic bombing of Japanese cities. However, Anscombe was not a Pacifist and in her essay "War and Murder" she explains why.

Firstly, Anscombe argues that Pacifism has nothing to do with Christianity and is based on a misinterpretation of Jesus and the New Testament. Anscombe argues that Jesus teaches us to go to great lengths to avoid violence and forbids immoral violence, but claims that Christianity does not oppose all violence all the time.

Secondly, Anscombe argues that instead of doing good, Pacifism actually causes harm. By telling us never to use violence, Pacifism sets too high a standard. This means that ordinary people end up respecting Pacifism, but feeling they cannot follow it in practice. Since they believe they cannot do what is best, Anscombe argues, then people end up feeling that it doesn't matter what they do in war and this is why atrocities happen. Anscombe explains why the Allied bombing of Hamburg and Dresden was morally wrong in this way:

"Now pacifism teaches people to make no distinction between the shedding of innocent blood and the shedding of any human blood ... hence seeing no way of avoiding wickedness, they set no limits to it."

For Anscombe, there is a vital difference between killing and murder. Murder is the killing of an innocent person, but in a war the enemy may not be innocent. This argument is considered in **JUST WAR THEORY** in a later chapter.

Anscombe's position is that of a Christian peacemaker, rather than a Pacifist. She sets high standards before she will agree that a war is moral, but not impossible standards. However, she opposes nuclear weapons because they make no distinction between the innocent and the guilty.

But is Anscombe correct that Pacifism leads to immorality when it fails to prevent war? Bomber Command, which led the raids on German cities, was led by Arthur "Bomber" Harris who was a Militarist or a Realist, but certainly not a Pacifist. Real Pacifists would argue that the people who carry out atrocities in war or make decisions to bomb civilians aren't Pacifists and aren't being influenced by Pacifism in any way.

It's difficult to decide on the truth of this, but Anscombe's argument should remind you that the Pacifist cannot have it both ways. If Pacifism has influenced the conduct of war in the 20th and 21st centuries then it might have influenced people to carry out atrocities too. If Pacifism has had no influence on the way war has been conducted, then Anscombe is wrong, but Pacifist protesters and Conscientious Objectors would also be wrong to claim they are doing some good during wartime.

DEONTOLOGY AND PACIFISM

Pacifists differ about whether war is instrumentally wrong (it is doomed to fail and will end up producing more misery than the other options, like diplomacy or surrender) or whether it is intrinsically wrong (it is evil and wrong even if it is successful). Deontological Pacifists believe war is intrinsically wrong. This means it is **NEVER** the right thing to go to war, no matter what the situation might be or what the consequences seem to be.

Deontological Pacifists are usually motivated by the moral duty not to kill other human beings. One type of Deontological Pacifism is **COSMOPOLITANISM** which views persons as citizens of the world, rather than of any particular country or nation. This global ethical viewpoint is supported by Soran Reader (2007) who defines cosmopolitan ethics as "the intuition that every human being has a moral status which constrains how they may be treated".

For Reader, cosmopolitanism implies strict Pacifism because of the indiscriminate nature of violence in war. She points out that when bombs are dropped, the pilot of the bomber has no idea which enemy soldiers will be injured or killed. Within a war, the enemy are treated as non-persons and this goes against Reader's Deontological view of how people must be treated.

Critics of Deontological Pacifism usually respond comparing war to killing in self-defence. Some Pacifists like Gandhi would say that even self-defence is no justification for killing another person. However, many people feel this to be an unfair moral rule. If someone attacks me and I'm not allowed to attack them back, then morality seems to be on the side of my attacker. The attacker can do anything to me, rob me or even kill me, and if I try to stop him using force then I'm the one in the wrong - how can that be fair?

This sort of contradiction is what the Deontologist philosopher Immanuel Kant calls a **CONTRADICTION IN NATURE**. This means that, once you try to universalise the law you are trying to obey, it leads to practical contradictions.

A similar criticism of Deontological Pacifism is that if someone has rights at all (for example, the right to life or to own property) then it makes no sense to say they have no right to enforce their rights. In what way do I have a "right to life" if I'm not allowed to stop anyone who tries to kill me - and nobody else is allowed to stop them either?

Immanuel Kant would call this a **CONTRADICTION IN THE WILL**. This is when you try to universalise the rule you are following and it leads to a contradiction with something else that you believe. It's impossible to want to live in that sort of world, because it can't really be imagined.

Many Deontological Pacifists make a different argument that applies specifically to war rather than self-defence. They say that the moral duty is not to kill **INNOCENT** human beings. A person who is trying to kill or rob you isn't innocent, but the people who just happen to live in an enemy country are innocent, especially if the enemy country isn't even a democracy so they didn't get a say in starting the war. Even if the enemy civilians do support their country's war effort, what about young children and babies living in the country?

This version of Deontological Pacifism seems to pass Kant's test for **UNIVERSALISABILITY**. When we are innocent, we don't want to be made to suffer for things that aren't our fault. It therefore follows that we shouldn't make other innocent people suffer for things that aren't their fault.

A lot of effort is made in modern war to avoid harming non-combatants in general. Technology like laser-guided missiles is used to pinpoint military targets. Despite this, civilians still get hurt and in shocking numbers. Additionally, some governments deliberately place civilians in the way of danger, creating "human shields" around their military bases. Some peace protesters even volunteer to join a human shield. The hope is that the risk of harming civilians will prevent an enemy from attacking that location. Forcing people to be part of a human shield is, of course, wrong - but it still leaves attackers with the problem of deciding to launch an attack which they know will kill innocents.

As a student of philosophy, you have to decide whether killing innocent people (and children and babies) can ever be morally acceptable.

AGAPE AND PACIFISM

Agape, or selfless love, would seem to support Pacifism. After all, what could be more loving than supporting peace and opposing war?

As discussed earlier, Agape is not about "warm fuzzy feelings". Dentists, surgeons, even executioners might act on Agape, even though they are causing pain or even killing someone. St Augustine of Hippo (354-440) argued that Agape demands that you do everything in your power to protect or rescue an innocent person, even if that means using force. However, Augustine rejected Absolute Pacifism and developed Just War Theory instead.

Joseph Fletcher, who pioneered Situation Ethics in the 1960s, gives another example of applying Agape to war. At the end of the Second World War, Japan refused to surrender to the Allies. The US Government considered a massive invasion of Japan itself, codenamed Operation Downfall. American forces would have had to cross the Pacific Ocean and launch the largest amphibian invasion in world history. It was estimated that American soldiers would suffer half a million casualties, but for the Japanese defending their homeland the casualties were estimated at 5-10 million.

Instead, the American President Truman chose to use the newly invented atomic bombs on the Japanese cities of Hiroshima and Nagasaki. When deciding whether to use "the most terrible weapon ever known" the President appointed a committee made up of top people in the government. Most of its military advisors favoured using it and so did Winston Churchill. Top-level scientists said they could find no acceptable alternative to using it, but other scientists disagreed. Eventually, the committee decided that the lives saved by ending the war swiftly outweighed the lives destroyed by using it.

Around 200,000 Japanese civilians died in the two attacks. Six days later, Japan surrendered. Today, Japan is a democratic and prosperous country and Article 9 of its constitution forbids any Japanese government from arming for war again.

Fletcher's point is not to show that the atomic bombing of Japanese cities was morally right (that is still very controversial) but to show that situations come up in war that can't be solved by Deontological rules. Instead you have to aim for the best outcome, wishing the best for your enemies. Many people wanted Japan to suffer for war crimes but instead the Americans helped rebuild Japan as a peaceful country that has never gone to war again. Fletcher suggests this was in fact the most loving thing to do in the situation. Sometimes you have to rescue a country from itself.

As a student of philosophy, you'll need to decide for yourself whether selfless love means never harming anyone or if moral rules can be broken in the name of selfless love. Situation Ethics seems to recommend a sort of **PACIFICISM** and you should ask yourself if a focus on Agape helps to remove the criticisms of Pacificism.

TELEOLOGY AND PACIFISM

Most Absolute Pacifists treat was as wrong without regard to the **CONSEQUENCES** of war or violence; they think war is intrinsically wrong. However some Pacifists argue that violence always leads to worse results than non-violence; they think war is instrumentally wrong. This is a Consequentialist position.

On the face of it, war clearly does lead inevitably to disastrous consequences: not just dead soldiers and bombed cities, but orphaned children, displaced refugees and follow-on problems like rape, looting, disease and mental health issues. Often these problems last for years after the war has come to an end.

Utilitarians are Consequentialists who insist that the consequences are ethically significant regardless of who they happen to, so the evil consequences for the enemy are just as morally important as the evil consequences for "our side". This means that even if your own country wins a crushing and casualty-free victory (say, by dropping an atom bomb on the enemy), the death, destruction and long-term suffering (eg radiation poisoning) for the enemy side still makes the war ethically wrong.

However, Consequentialists also have to weigh up the consequences of the alternatives to war before they can decide that war is wrong and this is where Consequentialist Pacifism runs into trouble. For one thing, the consequences are hard to calculate. What would the consequences have been for the Allies not to fight the Nazis? Some critics would say this instantly disqualifies Consequentialist Pacifism, but that seems to be going too far. After all, real governments really do try to weigh up the pros and cons before declaring war, so it's not unreasonable for moral philosophers to try to do the same.

A greater problem for Consequentialist Pacifism is when the alternatives to war all seem to lead to worse consequences than the war itself. The consequences of the Nazis conquering Europe unopposed would have been the enslavement of whole races and genocide on a grand scale. There's still room for disagreement here, because an Absolute Pacifist might want to claim that living in slavery is better than dying in war, but that's not something everyone will agree with - the Pacifist case has lost its obvious (prima facie) appeal.

Realists will point out that tyrants and dictators tend to view peacefulness as weakness, so, from a Consequentialist viewpoint, holding Pacifist views might make it more likely that warlike countries will launch invasions. This is similar to Thomas Hobbes' view that arming yourself to the teeth and showing that you mean business actually makes war less likely to happen.

Unless you are very strongly influenced by what Stephen Pinker calls the **UTOPIAN VISION** you probably can't base Absolute Pacifism on Consequentialism. This is because if we judge things solely in terms of consequences, killing people doesn't have to be wrong. Situations are imaginable where killing could lead to the best consequences. Consequentialist Pacifists are more likely to be drawn to Selective Pacifism (arguing that the consequences of using WMDs make wars unwinnable) or Pacificism (arguing that some wars are justifiable if the consequence is a more peaceful world afterwards).

As a student of philosophy, you will need to decide for yourself whether wars can ever bring about good consequences that outweigh all the pain and suffering they produce and what circumstances these might be.

ARETE AND PACIFISM

In the last chapter Aretaic Ethics were presented as strongly linked to Militarism, but what if the Virtuous Man is really a man of peace? Gandhi and Martin Luther King are widely seen as virtuous men and they advocated Pacifism. Most people think of **EUDAIMONIA** as living at peace with your neighbours in a peaceful society. Perhaps it follows that possessing and living the virtues involves promoting peace, both within yourself (developing a peaceful personality) and in society (opposing war).

Now it's clear that Aristotle himself didn't think about Arete in this way. In Ancient Greece military service was compulsory and Aristotle approved of it. The idea of the **GOLDEN MEAN** is against going to extremes, which seems to rule out Absolute Pacifism (which is quite an extreme view) but might approve of Selective Pacifism (which only objects to extreme weapons).

However, the world has changed a lot since Aristotle's time. In the Ancient World, war provided almost the only opportunity for young men to travel, meet new people, broaden their minds, bring back new ideas, exotic treasures and foreign brides. War enabled people from poor backgrounds to get rich or be promoted. Without war, societies tended to stagnate. War was necessary for Eudaimonia.

The modern world isn't like this. Young people today can go on package holidays to Cyprus or backpacking round Thailand. International business takes people to China or India all the time. You can come across new ideas and exotic goods on the Internet - in fact, you can get your foreign brides on the Internet too. There's no need to fight a war to get all the challenges and opportunities that war used to provide. In fact, a modern war would disrupt holidays and business, reducing Eudaimonia rather than increasing it. Possessing and living the virtues in the 21st C involves being a Pacifist rather than a Militarist.

One objection to this view of 21st C Arete is that it's intensely elitist. Only the most privileged people in the most privileged countries get to take gap years in Asia or safari holidays in Africa. Most people don't take business trips to Beijing; they do minimum wage jobs or work in sweatshops.

Virtue Ethics is often attacked for being elitist and Aristotle was certainly a snob as far as his views on women and slaves were concerned. However, modern ethics tries to be democratic. Immanuel Kant argues that the most important thing about ethics is universalisability - if something is good for you then you should wish everybody to do it and if that's not possible there's a **CONTRADICTION IN NATURE.** It doesn't seem to be possible for everyone to have gap years or work in globe-trotting jobs. On the other hand, for lots of young people without much of an education or a rich family behind them, the Armed Forces or the Territorial Army provides a chance to escape from unemployment or low-wage grind, travel, get trained and develop character.

As a student of philosophy, you will need to decide for yourself whether a commitment to peace is one of the virtues of not. If Pacifism is too extreme or else creates a frustrating life for ordinary people, it can't lead to Eudaimonia. On the other hand, 2300 years on from Aristotle, perhaps the world needs new virtues based on peace rather than war.

CHRISTIANITY AND PACIFISM

Many people view Christianity as a religion of peace - Christians even refer to Jesus as the "Prince of Peace". In the Bible, Jesus recommends peace on many occasions:

> *"Blessed are the peacemakers, for they shall be called sons of God" - Matthew 5: 9*

> *"Do not resist an evil person. If anyone slaps you on the right cheek, turn the other cheek to them also" - Matthew 5: 39*

> *"If you forgive men when they sin against you, your Heavenly Father will also forgive you" - Matthew 6: 14*

Jesus also behaves like a Pacifist by not resisting the soldiers when they come to arrest him and telling his followers not to fight to defend him. This example was followed by the Early Christians who refused to join the Roman Army. During the anti-Christian persecutions by several Roman Emperors, Christians allowed themselves to be taken to execution without resisting. Some people conclude from this that Christianity was originally a Pacifist religion and later Christian Militarism is actually a perversion of Jesus' message.

Other Christians, such as Elizabeth Anscombe, disagree with this interpretation. For one thing, Jesus' teachings about peace seem to have a domestic context, not a military one. He is talking about people quarrelling with their families, neighbours and servants, not war. As evidence for this, critics like Anscombe point out that, when Jesus has the opportunity to criticise soldiers (like the Centurion in Matthew 8: 5-13) he doesn't tell them to quit their jobs.

Of course it might be that Jesus did in fact criticise these jobs, but the Gospels don't mention it. They might not mention it because they thought it was too obvious to need mentioning or because they didn't want to present Jesus as "anti-Roman" when they were trying to convert people in the Roman Empire.

Anscombe also points out that the Early Christians were not Pacifists in the modern sense. They believed the Roman Empire was ruled by demons and that the Day of Judgement was coming soon. You don't join the army if you believe your country is evil and doomed anyway. The Early Christians wanted more than anything to be martyrs so they could join Jesus in Heaven. You don't fight against your attackers if you actually want them to kill you. But after 300 years of Christianity, the Day of Judgement seemed as far off as ever and the Roman Empire had converted to Christianity. Now that the Empire was no longer evil and didn't seem to be doomed, Christians started fighting to defend it. This would suggest they were never Absolute Pacifists in the first place.

Despite these arguments, many Christians view Jesus' life as a life dedicated to peace and it is a life they feel obliged to imitate. Some Christian groups (eg Quakers, Jehovah's Witnesses) believe there is a religious duty to be a Conscientious Objector. Many other Christians believe that overcoming violence, even if it leads to self-destruction, is a necessary transformation to become Christ-like. This is sometimes called **PARTICULAR PACIFISM**, because religious believers think God expects them particularly to stay out of war, but do not necessarily condemn everyone else for fighting in a war.

Most other Christians agree that war is an evil thing, but not necessarily the most evil. They argue that preventing even greater evils can justify a Christian fighting in a war. This view of war as a necessary evil is called Just War Theory.

If you are studying philosophy from a Christian perspective, you will need to decide for yourself whether the idea of a "Christian Pacifist" is supported by Jesus' life and teachings and, if so, what sort of Pacifism a Christian is supposed to uphold.

THE PACIFIST'S LETTER OF LAST RESORT

If the British Prime Minister were a Pacifist, what instruction would they put in the Letter of Last Resort?

Pacifists see a negative value in war and a nuclear war that destroys human civilisation (or even the human species) is unjustifiable. Consequentialist Pacifists argue that war never produces good outcomes for people, but a nuclear war leaves no people to enjoy any sort of outcomes, good or bad. Deontological Pacifists object to the death of innocents as a matter of principle, and launching the missiles would cause this.

Moreover, the sorts of Pacifists who sometimes endorse war (Defencists, Pacificists and Selective Pacifists) would be forced to agree with the Absolute Pacifists. Defencists will endorse war as a way of defending their country, but in this scenario Britain has been destroyed so there is no longer a country to defend. Pacificists endorse war that promotes global peace, but there need to be survivors to enjoy that peace, which a nuclear Armageddon makes unlikely. Most Selective Pacifists reject the use of nuclear weapons anyway.

It is unthinkable that a Pacifist would order the submarine captains to retaliate, but this leaves two further questions: which of the other three options would the Pacifist choose?

Leaving the choice to the captains is risky. As important Naval officers, there's a good chance they are Militarists or Realists. As we have seen, this doesn't necessarily make them any more likely to launch the missiles either, but shock and anger might overwhelm their good judgement. Ordinarily, Defencists and Pacificists would be happy to send the submarines to a friendly power, but this scenario is complicated for them because the nuclear deterrent has already failed once (it didn't protect Britain) and if they don't order a retaliation this time, then there's no reason why it should ever work again, because it will be shown to be an empty bluff.

The dilemma the Pacifists face is, what can be done with a weapon that is unethical to use but cannot be un-invented? One bold solution is Unilateral Disarmament. Unilateral means "one-sided"; this is where a country dismantles its nuclear weapons regardless of what other countries decide to do. Many Pacifists believe that such a gesture would break the tense stand-off between nuclear powers and encourage others to dismantle their nuclear weapons too. A Pacifist Prime Minister who believed this could instruct the submarines not to retaliate then announce to the world that this is what has been done.

There's a gamble in this strategy. Realists would argue that when one country acts unpredictably, for reasons of morality, it upsets the carefully-laid plans of their rivals and enemies, making war more likely. Moreover, even if a later Prime Minister changed the letter and went back to secrecy (or announced that it instructed retaliation), a seed of doubt has been sown. Other countries will wonder if Britain is telling the truth, if there is any serious intention of using the nuclear missiles. The deterrent will never again work as well as it did.

On the other hand, believers in Agape and Arete might support this approach as the only way to break out of a nuclear standoff based on bluff and deception. Agape demands a level of honesty in relationships and Arete opposes basing safety and security on deceit. For Christian ethicists, a supernatural belief in the Holy Spirit might reassure them that this sort of gamble will not misfire. Secular Pacifists will need a very strong faith in what Stephen Pinker calls the **UTOPIAN VISION**, that rival countries will not interpret morality as weakness.

KEY TERMS

- **ABSOLUTE PACIFISM**

- **CONSCIENTIOUS OBJECTOR**

- **CONSEQUENTIALIST PACIFISM**

- **DEFENCISM**

- **DEONTOLOGICAL PACIFISM**

- **FREE RIDER**

- **PACIFISM**

- **SELECTIVE PACIFISM**

- **UTOPIAN VISION**

SELF-ASSESSMENT QUESTIONS

1. Explain what is good about peace.

2. Outline the strengths and weaknesses of Pacifism as an ethical philosophy.

3. What would be a Pacificist (as distinct from Pacifist, see text) interpretation of a conflict in the world today?

4. "It's all a long way away and it's none of our business." Is this a reasonable statement of Defencism? What's wrong with it?

5. Is Pacifism unworldly? Does it matter?

6. Does Pacifism involve rejecting all violence or only war? What's

the difference?

7. To what extent is the Bible a Pacifist text?

8. Is Elizabeth Anscombe right in arguing that there's a difference between war and murder? Why?

9. Is there a moral problem with nuclear deterrence if it works?

10. When good men do nothing, does evil win?

FURTHER READING

- **ANSCOMBE, GEM** - War and Murder (1961), originally printed in Stein, W. (ed.), Nuclear Weapons (1961) but available online

- **DOWER, N** - The Ethics of War & Peace (2009), Polity, Ch 5

- **FIALA, A** - Practical Pacifism (2008), Algora, Ch 3

- **NORMAN, R** - Ethics, Killing & War (1995), Cambridge, Ch 6

- **OREND, B** - The Morality of War (2006), Broadview, Ch 9

- **TEICHMAN, J** - Pacifism & The Just War (1986), Blackwell

- **WALTZER, M** - Just & Unjust Wars (1977), Basic Books, Afterword

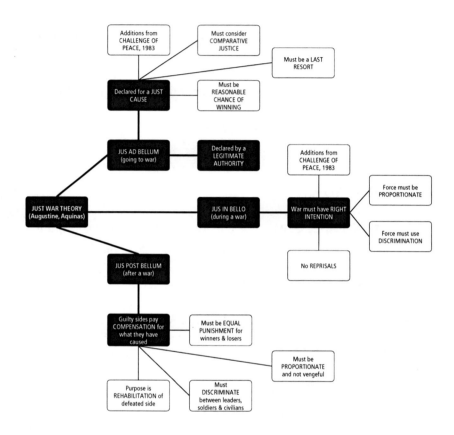

Additions from CHALLENGE OF PEACE, 1983

Must consider COMPARATIVE JUSTICE

Must be a LAST RESORT

Declared for a JUST CAUSE

Must be REASONABLE CHANCE OF WINNING

JUS AD BELLUM (going to war)

Declared by a LEGITIMATE AUTHORITY

Additions from CHALLENGE OF PEACE, 1983

Force must be PROPORTIONATE

JUST WAR THEORY (Augustine, Aquinas)

JUS IN BELLO (during a war)

War must have RIGHT INTENTION

Force must use DISCRIMINATION

No REPRISALS

JUS POST BELLUM (after a war)

Guilty sides pay COMPENSATION for what they have caused

Must be EQUAL PUNISHMENT for winners & losers

Must be PROPORTIONATE and not vengeful

Purpose is REHABILITATION of defeated side

Must DISCRIMINATE between leaders, soldiers & civilians

Just War Theory

"The commandment forbidding killing was not broken by those who have waged wars on the authority of God, or those who have imposed the death-penalty on criminals when representing the authority of the state." - Augustine of Hippo

WAR AS A NECESSARY EVIL

Militarism views war as a good thing, Realism views it as a necessary thing and Pacifism views it as an evil thing, but there is another position to take. This is the view that war is a necessary evil. As you can see, this combines some of the thinking of Pacifism (that it would be better if there were no war) and Realism (that, since the world is the way it is, wars will continue to happen).

If war is a necessary evil, then we can distinguish between Just Wars (which are necessary) and Unjust Wars (which are not). But what exactly makes a war necessary? We must be careful here, because if "necessary" just means "unavoidable" then we have adopted a Realist position. Every war is avoidable if you refuse to fight. By "necessary" we mean "morally necessary" - refusing to fight would not be weak or irrational, it would actually be morally wrong. So a Just War is a war where the alternatives are morally worse than the war itself. A Just War isn't simply a war which is morally excusable; it's a war which would be morally wrong NOT to fight.

There is a long history of Just War thinking, from Ancient Greece and Rome (Plato, Aristotle, Cicero, Seneca) through to the Renaissance (Hugo Grotius) and the Enlightenment (Jeremy Bentham). Nevertheless, Just War Theory is often associated with Christian ethics, especially Roman Catholic ethics.

Although the Early Christians refused to fight their enemies, by the 4th C Christianity was the official religion of the Roman Empire. Now that the Empire was a Christian Empire, it needed to be defended against barbarians (who were either pagans or Christian heretics) and neighbouring empires (the Persians, who were Zoroastrian by religion and persecuted Christians even more enthusiastically than the Romans had). What was needed was some idea of the "Christian soldier" - an unthinkable concept for the early Christians. The idea was introduced by Ambrose of Milan but developed by his more famous student Augustine of Hippo. Augustine suggested that a Christian soldier might fight in a Just War.

Augustine wrote in the 4th C when the Roman Empire in the West was collapsing. Emperors were being assassinated and rival generals battled for control. Barbarians poured into the Empire, either as invaders or refugees, and carved out new kingdoms. Law and order were breaking down and the Christian Church faced the problem of heresies - unusual varieties of Christianity that were popular among the barbarians driving traditional Christianity underground. From Augustine's home in North Africa (modern Algeria) it seemed like the end of civilisation itself.

Augustine's solution was to call on Christians to fight for the Empire and defend civilisation. However, he had to be careful. Among all the chaos, bandits and rebels were setting themselves up as warlords and Augustine didn't want to defend an "anything goes" approach to war. He sought to justify war but condemn lawless mayhem and killing.

JUS AD BELLUM

This means the justice of **GOING TO** war, sometimes called "Just Cause".

- A Just War can only be declared by a "legitimate authority".

- A Just War must be fought in support of a "just cause".

Augustine was clear that only the Emperor (or one of his official representatives) had the right to start a war and that war should be fought to punish wrongdoing and defend the Empire, not just to grab territory or settle old scores. Anyone else raising an army or attacking their neighbours was engaged in unjust warfare.

Augustine has a fairly specific idea of Jus Ad Bellum in mind (fighting to hold the Roman Empire together) but his ideas continued to be influential long after the Roman Empire had collapsed. In the Middle Ages, Thomas Aquinas (1225-1274) was deeply inspired by Augustine and restated the importance of Jus Ad Bellum. This time the problems were different - feuding barons and squabbles between royal families threatened to tear Christian Europe apart.

The Roman Catholic Church tried to limit some of the destruction by insisting that a war was only just if the Pope approved of it. For example, in 1066, William of Normandy received Pope Alexander II's approval for his war to claim the English throne that had been promised to him. The Pope blessed a flag and sent it to William to lead his army, making his invasion of England a Just War. Of course, this also shows the problem with Jus Ad Bellum, because King Harold of England refused to recognise that the Pope was a "legitimate authority" over his country. For Harold and his English knights, the Norman invaders were carrying out an Unjust War. Historians still debate about who was right.

Today, people still appeal to a "legitimate authority" in war. Many people believe the United Nations is this sort of authority. For example, the United Nations gave its approval to the USA in 1950 to fight to protect South Korea from North Korean invasion. This led to the Korean War. The United Nations also approved "peacekeeping missions" in countries like El Salvador and Mozambique. The United Nations also condemns some wars, like the Syrian government's behaviour in the Syrian Civil War and many military actions taken by Israel against its neighbours.

However, there are problems with looking to the United Nations to legitimise a war, because the United Nations does not have complete authority over what countries do. The United Nations did not give its approval to the American-led invasions of Afghanistan in 2001 and Iraq in 2003. The USA and UK governments claim that no approval was needed in these cases, but critics argue that, without United Nations approval, these invasions were "illegal wars".

The whole idea of Jus Ad Bellum is difficult to interpret and there is rarely complete agreement. However, the idea of an "illegal war" comes from the concept of a Just War and this is an important part of modern moral thinking about war. "Just cause" is easier to define. For Augustine, a just cause is self-defence, recovering what has been stolen and punishing wrongdoers. Again, Augustine is imagining Roman legions teaching barbarian raiders a lesson. A modern definition from the US Catholic Conference (1993) is:

> "... to correct a grave, public evil, ie, aggression or massive violation of the basic rights of whole populations."

This seems to justify using war to prevent genocide but could also include invasions to root out terrorists or end slavery. Michael Waltzer

(1977) writes about a Just War aiming to put a stop to events which

"... shock the moral conscience of mankind."

There is a vagueness about these definitions, because not all of mankind finds the same things shocking or agrees on what "basic rights" should be. Is another country assassinating one of your leaders a just cause for war? Or how about insulting your state religion? We will look in more detail at one of the more controversial acts of war that is sometimes defended as a just cause: the pre-emptive strike.

PRE-EMPTIVE STRIKES

An important issue with the whole idea of Jus Ad Bellum is whether or not you have to wait for someone to attack you before you're allowed to attack them.

If you do wait for an enemy to attack you first, you'll definitely have Just Cause to attack them back. However, you'll also be at a huge disadvantage when you try to do it. The enemy's attacks might have destroyed your military bases and factories or captured strategic sites like airports. The enemy attack might even have caused massive civilian casualties, especially if it used WMDs. In fact a "first strike" can be so devastating there is nothing the other country can do in self-defence afterwards.

An alternative is the "pre-emptive strike" - attacking them before they get to attack you. The United Nations forbids pre-emptive strikes unless they have been specially approved by the United Nations itself. According to Waltzer (1977), Just War Theory is rather more generous, allowing a pre-emptive strike when there is:

> *"... a manifest intent to injure, a degree of active preparation that makes that intent a positive danger, and a general situation in which waiting, or doing anything other than fighting, greatly magnifies the risk."*

The USA claims it had Just Cause to launch a pre-emptive strike on Afghanistan and Iraq as part of its War On Terror. In effect, the USA needed to attack those countries in order to defend itself from more attacks like the World Trade Center bombing in 2001 (9/11) and doing anything other than attacking the country where Al-Qaeda was based would have "magnified the risk".

Sometimes pre-emptive strikes are targeted at specific locations. For example, in 1981 bombers from Israel flew over Iraq and destroyed a nuclear reactor that Israel believed was being used to make nuclear weapons. Once the reactor was destroyed the bombers flew home. The United Nations condemned the attack but Israel argued it had Just Cause because Iraq had acquired nuclear weapons it would have used them to threaten Israel; in other words there was "active preparation" based on "intent to injure". Israel launched a similar pre-emptive strike against a nuclear reactor in Syria in 2007.

JUS IN BELLO

Augustine also added that Jus in Bello is important too; this Latin phrase means the justice how you **GO ABOUT** war.

Augustine suggested Christian soldiers must feel no hatred towards their enemies in war and must maintain virtuous feelings while killing. From a non-religious viewpoint, this isn't very important (most of us don't care how soldiers feel about us while they're bombing our homes) but Augustine's ideas were developed further by Thomas Aquinas who added a third requirement for a war to be a Just War.

A Just War must have right intention

In a way, this is just taking Augustine's idea that Christian soldiers must not love killing for its own sake and making it a general rule - Just Wars are not only in support of a "just cause", they are also carried out in a moral way (accepting the other side's surrender, sparing civilians and prisoners, or honouring truces). The war must be fought purely in pursuit of the Just Cause and once that has been achieved the war must end. There will be temptations to settle old scores, grab territory, displace certain ethnic groups or prevent retaliations through striking terror into the enemy population, but if you do these things you do not have Right Intention.

An example of this might be the behaviour of the German Government at the start of the Second World War. It could be argued that Hitler was, at the time, a "legitimate authority" and reuniting the historic German territories that had been split up after the First World War was (to many Germans) a "just cause". However, the Nazis grabbed much wider territories than this and put whole populations into concentration camps, driving out or enslaving Jewish, Gypsy and Slavic communities. This showed they did not have Right Intention.

One of the features of Just War Theory is that it is all-or-nothing. You cannot have a partially just war. If a war fails to meet one of the conditions (eg lack of Right Intention) then it is unjust, no matter what the cause is or who legitimised it.

On the other hand, Right Intention can be very difficult to judge, especially in a war. The Nazis famously kept their instructions vague - even a phrase like "the Final Solution" (meaning the Holocaust) is imprecise. This means that leaders can always say afterwards that their instructions were misunderstood by their soldiers and it was never their intention that massacres and atrocities should take place. International law does not refer to Right Intention when deciding whether a war is legal or illegal. Something more precise is needed.

THE CHALLENGE OF PEACE

In 1983 the Catholic Bishops in America issued a statement The Challenge of Peace updating the criterion for a Just War. Based on the wars of the 20th C, they added new conditions.

Two of them are related to Jus Ad Bellum:

1. **COMPARATIVE JUSTICE** - You must consider the justice of the other side's claims, rather than assuming you are automatically in the right.

2. **WAR MUST BE A LAST RESORT** - Every diplomatic avenue must be exhausted first. Sending soldiers to die in a campaign that's clearly doomed from the start is also wrong.

The others are related to Jus In Bello:

1. **PROBABILITY OF SUCCESS** - Refusing to surrender and fighting to the death (as Hitler did at the end of World War Two) is immoral; if a war can no longer be won it should be ended.

2. **PROPORTIONALITY** - The suffering caused by the war must be in proportion to the injustice that started it, so it would be wrong for a rich, powerful country to start a war with a poor, weak country over a minor border dispute or drop a nuclear bomb on a country in a war over fishing rights.

3. **DISCRIMINATION** - Civilian casualties must be minimised as far as possible and tactics like starvation or rape cannot be used as weapons of war.

4. **NO REPRISALS** - The war effort must be focused on winning

the war, not revenge. Just because the enemy has broken the rules of Jus In Bello it doesn't mean your soldiers can "teach them a lesson" by breaking the rules in return.

The Challenge of Peace was written at the height of the Cold War, with the USA and the Soviet Union threatening each other with nuclear weapons. It probably seemed to the authors that this would go on forever, so they don't take a Pacifist view on nuclear weapons or nuclear war. Ten years later, the Cold War had ended and the Soviet Union no longer existed. This is a good example of a problem with Just War Theory - it accepts that war is inevitable and necessary, when perhaps we should try to stop it altogether.

COLLATERAL DAMAGE

One of the biggest problems for Just War Theory is the problem of **COLLATERAL DAMAGE**. This is when weapons of war cause harm to civilians, especially to civilians who are nothing to do with the war effort (eg children). This can happen directly when bombs aimed at military targets fall on homes and schools. It can happen indirectly when the war causes lack of food and medicine and civilians die of starvation and disease.

Civilians are off-limits as far as Just War Theory is concerned and international law agrees with this. Harming civilians shows a lack of Right Intention; specifically, it shows a lack of the discrimination needed for Jus In Bello.

Modern military technology has come a long way in this regard. Laser-guided missiles can pinpoint military targets in the middle of a crowded street. Nevertheless, there is still collateral damage when bystanders are hurt. When soldiers invade, the potential for collateral damage increases. In the heat of battle, with confusion and chaos all round, discipline can break down and atrocities can occur. A notorious example is the My Lai Massacre in 1968, when Charlie Company, a group of American soldiers fighting in the Vietnam War, massacred a village of peaceful Vietnamese civilians on the suspicion they might be supporting enemy troops. Prisoners were shot, others beaten and mutilated and women were raped.

There are less extreme examples. A key part of any future war will by cyber-warfare, which means using computer hacking to disable an enemy's computer systems. This will of course make it hard for an enemy country to fly its jets or navigate its tanks. It will also cut off telephone systems that civilians use or make it hard for hospitals to treat patients.

A computer virus can be a weapon of war, but it's highly indiscriminate because computer systems are linked together and affect everyone.

Militarists and Realists might argue that no one is really innocent in war. Merely by being "on the Other Side" civilians are part of the enemy state and therefore are "fair game". They might still try to reduce collateral damage - Militarists might do this because they are honourable, Realists because collateral damage enrages the enemy and makes it more likely they will try to harm your civilians.

Just War philosophers cannot take this view. Harming innocents makes a war an Unjust War and therefore wrong. Innocents cannot be "fair game".

A Pacifist view is that this shows the failure of Just War Theory. If collateral damage cannot be prevented and if collateral damage is unjustifiable, then every war is an Unjust War, which is what Absolute Pacifists believe.

DOUBLE EFFECT

Just War Theory has a traditional answer to the problem of harming innocents during war. The Catholic term for this argument is the Doctrine of Double Effect (**DDE**). Similar arguments are also used by non-Catholic supporters of Just War.

Double Effect is the idea that whenever we take an action it produces two sorts of consequences, things we intended and things we don't intend. These are the "double effects" of our actions. We are morally responsible for the effects that are intentional, but not for the effects we didn't intend. So if you undertake an action with the best of intentions (like blowing up a bridge to stop enemy tanks crossing it) and this leads to effects you never intended (like preventing an ambulance getting across it to save a sick child) then the action is still a good action.

Many people think this way in ordinary life. We use phrases like "it's the thought that counts" or "her heart was in the right place".

Double Effect would seem to permit Just Wars, so long as the people fighting to take every effort to reduce civilian casualties. According to the DDE, if innocent people are harmed as a result of the unintended side-effects of war, then this still allows a war to be a Just War.

There are some qualifications to the DDE.

1. The action itself must be morally acceptable - Just War Theory is not a Consequentialist theory of war and you can't justify doing something terrible (like genocide) based on the idea that end justifies the means.

2. You must genuinely intend only the good effects and not the bad side-effects. Civilian deaths do demoralise the enemy and

Realists might aim to kill civilians in order to increase pressure on the enemy to surrender. However, Just War philosophers cannot approve of this. You must minimise civilian casualties no matter how helpful they might be.

3. Finally, the unintended side-effects must be actual side-effects, not necessary steps that bring about the intended effect. For example, when President Truman ordered atom bombs to be dropped on Hiroshima and Nagasaki his intended effect was that Japan would surrender and the war would end - a good intention. However, the deaths of 200,000 Japanese civilians were NOT an unintended side-effect of dropping the atomic bombs. They were the very means that would bring about the surrender of Japan. If the bombs had gone off harmlessly and no one had died, Japan would not have surrendered. Those deaths were necessary for the President's intentions to come about. Therefore the DDE cannot be used to excuse the use of atom bombs against Japan in 1945 (or the British bombing of Dresden that year).

Michael Waltzer (1992) sums up the DDE position by saying that governments must give "due care" to the protection of civilians in war. So long as "due care" is being taken, a war can be a Just War even though there are innocent deaths.

Absolute Pacifists will not be happy with the "due care" argument, which seems to be saying that there's nothing wrong with killing innocent people so long as you tried your hardest not to. A Pacifist can easily reply that 'trying your hardest' means not going to war in the first place. Anyone actually dropping bombs on enemy cities clearly has not "tried their hardest".

Realists and Militarists will also criticise "due care" because it involves putting your own soldiers at a disadvantage and possibly prolonging the war. Although the bombing of Dresden was terrible, the Nazis were determined never to surrender and the bombing speeded up the Allied advance on Berlin and the end of the war.

Other critics see problems with the DDE as a whole. It is common to focus on the distinction, important for defenders of the DDE, between **FORSEEING** an evil and **INTENDING** that evil. This distinction is not easy to explain.

For example, if a soldier throws himself on top of a live grenade, he sacrifices his own life to save his comrades. Most defenders of the DDE would say this is well-intentioned and morally permissible. Yet it is rather implausible to say that the soldier only foresees that he might die as a side-effect of this. Surely he actually intends to die heroically (which many Catholic defenders of the DDE believe is the same as suicide and morally wrong).

A similar argument can be made for killing in self-defence or defence of others. If a maniac attacks me and I save myself by shooting him in the head, how is it meaningful to say I only foresaw, but never intended, his death? Surely his death was precisely what I intended. This is particularly important because the analogy with killing in defence is a key part of Just War Theory.

Furthermore, Consequentialists oppose the whole idea of judging the morality of an action by its motives. John Stuart Mill (1863) sums up the problems with the DDE like this:

"He who saves a fellow creature from drowning does what is morally right, whether his motive be duty, or the hope of being paid for his trouble; he who betrays the friend that trusts him, is guilty of a crime, even if his object be to serve another friend to whom he is under greater obligations."

ARGUING AGAINST JUST WAR THEORY

Philosophers have had mixed feelings about the whole concept of a "Just War". Some point out that Augustine and Aquinas introduced a valuable idea into warfare - that there were moral rules governing war rather than just might-makes-right. During the Middle Ages the Church supported truces and ceasefires and encouraged knights to feel guilty about at least some of the killing they had done.

Others think it is very regrettable that Christianity moved from being a religion of peace to one that was willing to endorse war; maybe the idea of a "Just War" actually creates more wars. When people think that wars are morally justified, they might be keen to start them. However, Just War Theory insists that war is a necessary **EVIL** - something tragic to be avoided and regretted. Regarding war as something good is a Militarist rather than a Just War viewpoint.

Just War Theory demands that a war meets all its conditions for Jus Ad Bellum and Jus In Bello but it's worth asking yourself if any war in history has actually met all these conditions. Has there ever been a truly Just War? If there never has been a Just War, then in practice Just War Theory amounts to Pacifism.

- First of all, consider the need for a "just cause". This is clearly open to interpretation and everybody waging a war thinks their cause is just - Palestinians firing rockets into Israeli suburbs, Taleban insurgents planting bombs at the roadside, Irish republicans blowing up crowded pubs, Nazi stormtroopers rounding up Jewish families, American marines napalming Vietnamese farmers: everyone thinks they're fighting in a just cause. Even St Augustine's idea that it was just to defend the Empire and its laws only seemed just to Roman citizens; the barbarians desperately trying to carve out a new home for themselves wouldn't have seen the justice in it.

- "Legitimate authority" is equally hard to define. Did Tony Blair and George W Bush have the authority to declare war on Iraq in 2003? Many people today think that only the United Nations should have the authority to approve a war, but at the moment that isn't the case. Nevertheless, there are some who accuse Bush and Blair of being "war criminals" and view the invasion as an "illegal war".

- "Right intention" can be just as vague, particularly because what leaders say is their motive and aim in going to war and then what actually ends up happening can be quite different. Britain and America say it is their intention to set up peaceful democracies in Iraq and Afghanistan and then leave, but many people (particularly in the Muslim world) distrust these intentions and think that the real intention is to control the supply of oil or even to eradicate Islam as a religion. It doesn't matter whether these accusations are true or not, it just shows that "right intention" is not something everyone can agree on.

- "Comparative justice" is a very weak condition, because there is always justice on both sides in any dispute. The Nazis had a case that the Versailles Treaty was unfair and the division of their territory was damaging to them as a people. Saddam Hussein had a point that Iraq wasn't harbouring WMDs or supporting al-Qaeda as American and British leaders claimed. However, countries can never admit that their enemies have some justice on their side, because it would weaken their own standing internationally.

The demand that war should be a "last resort" has a lot of support, but just how far is diplomacy expected to go? In March 2003 the US government announced that "diplomacy had failed" to get Saddam Hussein to comply with United Nations Security Resolutions and the invasion of Iraq began a few days later. But many people believe Iraq needed more time to comply with UN Resolution 1441 and that the United Nations needed to debate the matter further. Who can say when diplomacy really has failed, as opposed to leaders simply losing patience?

Other conditions are less problematic.

- "Reasonable probability of success" is important because, although last stands by doomed soldiers in the face of overwhelming odds make for romantic stories ("Remember the Alamo!"), it is irrational and wicked for leaders, from the safety of their palaces and bunkers, to send people to die in a hopeless struggle.

- "Proportionality" is also not very controversial. For example, defending national honour is very important for some people, but the lives of human beings should take priority over national honour.

- "Discrimination" is another important idea, but one that has been discussed in the preceding section on Collateral Damage.

A deeper problem arises with defining who is "innocent" in war. Groups like Hamas and Hezbollah don't make a distinction between "innocent" or "guilty" Israelis - Israelis are all, collectively, seen as guilty of occupying Arab land and mistreating the Arab population; Israeli civilians are considered legitimate targets for suicide bombers or random missiles.

Just War Theory has traditionally rejected this belief, focusing on the ethics of soldiers fighting other soldiers. But not all wars are like this. Some Palestinians regard the state of Israel as oppressing them simply by existing. Their objection is not just to Israeli soldiers, but to Israel itself. This is a dilemma faced by nationalist groups in other parts of the world, like Basques in Spain or Tamils in Sri Lanka. If you don't officially have a country, how can you "declare war" on your enemy? Civil wars in particular produce situations where no one is an innocent bystander and challenge some of the key assumptions of Just War Theory.

JUS POST BELLUM

More recently, a refinement to Just War theory has been to think about the ethics of victory: how should the defeated country be treated morally? Reinhold Niebuhr (1934) famously argued that the cause of the Second World War lay in the unjust Versailles Treaty that concluded the First World War and even Prime Minister Lloyd George later observed:

> *"Was it sensible to treat her as a cow from which to extract milk and beef at the same time?"*

To avoid history repeating itself the Allies carefully (and expensively) rebuilt both Germany and Japan after the Second World War. Ironically, this meant that Germany and Japan quickly became more prosperous than victorious countries like Britain. Although the US and British-led coalition conquered Iraq and Afghanistan with military force, critics say they failed to deliver Jus Post Bellum. The brutal behaviour of some troops, the corruption of new leaders and a sense of grievance produced a terrorist insurgency that was much more bloody than the original war.

Jus Post Bellum involves the following issues:

1. **PROPORTIONALITY** - The settlement at the end of the war must not be unduly harsh (as many people think the Versailles Treaty was for defeated Germany in 1919) or based on revenge. This includes the idea that it is wrong to demand the enemy's unconditional surrender (the way the Allies demanded the unconditional surrender of the Nazis).

2. **EQUAL PUNISHMENT** - War crimes should be dealt with, but crimes committed by BOTH sides must be investigated. The

winning side cannot simply forgive its own soldiers for any atrocities or abuses.

3. **COMPENSATION** - The guilty side in a war should compensate its victims, paying to repair structural damage or support invalids, widows and orphans created by the war

4. **DISCRIMINATION** - Punishments should fall on leaders first, soldiers second and civilians last, if at all. Innocents caught up in the war should not be made to suffer after it. This includes the idea that it is wrong to strip a defeated country of its wealth to pay for the cost of defeating it - this only stirs up resentment making a future war more likely.

5. **REHABILITATION** - The defeated country may need to be rebuilt and its leaders retrained, especially if its institutions (racist beliefs, religious fanaticism, militaristic codes of conduct) helped start the war in the first place. In post-war Germany and Japan rehabilitation created peaceful democratic countries that rejected the sort of aggression that had previously been admired.

Jus Post Bellum is often unpopular with the public on the winning side, especially if they feel they didn't start the war and lost loved ones and suffered hardships in order to win it. The public often feels that the losing side deserves to be humiliated and punished; it is the tricky job of Just War philosophers to argue that this normal feeling is, in fact, immoral.

Jus Post Bellum is often no more popular with the losing side, who can resent the victors' justice or see it as no justice at all. It may be many years before anyone can look back and see that what was done was done fairly.

Rehabilitation is particularly controversial. Sometimes the losing country resents being rehabilitated and sees this as having an alien and unwanted culture imposed on it by foreigners. This sort of attitude seems to have made Jus Post Bellum difficult in Afghanistan, where some groups continue to use violence to oppose educating women, democratic voting or human rights. Rehabilitation can involve spreading evil institutions rather than dismantling them. For example, the Nazis encouraged anti-Semitism in the countries they conquered, spreading their cruel ideology.

THE RULES OF WAR

One of the practical effects of Just War Theory has been to develop codes of conduct for nations at war. As we have seen, the Militarist might agree to these codes out of a sense of honour and the Realist might agree to them for more selfish reasons, calculating that his own prisoners and civilians will be better treated if he respects these rules too.

The First **GENEVA CONVENTION** in 1864 obliged warring armies to respect medical staff. The Red Cross was recognised as a neutral medical group. Britain and the USA signed this Convention soon after.

The Second and Third Geneva Conventions in the early 20th C laid down rules to protect seamen, victims of shipwreck and prisoners of war. The 1925 Protocol banned the use of poison gas.

The most complete statement of the rules of war, and the one most people think of as "the Geneva Convention" was the Fourth Geneva Convention of 1949 which adds rules to protect civilians during war.

In 1997 more protocols were added to recognise that guerrillas are soldiers deserving rights and adding rules to protect people taking part in "wars of national liberation". Before this, governments could argue that guerrillas and rebels were criminals, not soldiers, and possibly execute them. The 1997 Protocol is more controversial than the rest since it can be interpreted to protect terrorists. Militarists might argue that terrorism is dishonourable and rebellion is treasonous and the public often supports treating such people very harshly.

Since 1993, the United Nations has declared that any countries engaged in war are subject to the Geneva Conventions, whether or not they signed up to them. Countries that violate the Conventions break International Law.

For most Just War Theorists the development of the Geneva Conventions is a major step forward in defining what is a War Crime and making conflict more humane. Pacifists will have a more complex view, since by defining what counts as a War Crime these Conventions suggest that everything else that happens in war is morally acceptable. Absolute Pacifists would disagree with this, since they define all war as criminal and immoral.

CASE STUDY: THE VIETNAM WAR

It will be helpful to look at this war as a brief case study to analyse it in terms of Just War Theory, so that the Theory's principles can be seen in action.

Vietnam had been a French colony called Indochina that achieved independence after the Second World War. At this time Communism was immensely popular in Asia and Vietnam's neighbour, China, had recently undergone a Communist revolution. Some of the Vietnamese wished to follow China. These Vietnamese Communists, or Vietcong, were based in Hanoi in the north and led by Ho Chi Minh. In the south a democratic government existed, supported by America and based in Saigon. In 1954 the Geneva Agreement divided the country along the 17th parallel, with the Vietcong to the north. The southern government carried out a referendum on the future of the country, but fixed the voting so that the leader, Ngo Dinh Diem, could declare himself president. As a result, the country slipped into a civil war.

America had been supporting Diem's government with money, arms and training, but in the 1963 Ngo Dinh Diem was assassinated. By now the government in the South was very unpopular and the Vietcong were ready to take over. American Presidents started sending more and more troops to bases in Vietnam. In 1964 the Vietcong attacked Camp Holloway, a US military base in the South. The USA retaliated with more bombing and the Vietcong with more attacks until the US launched Operation Rolling Thunder, a campaign of continuous bombing of Viet Cong bases and civilian communities in the North. The USA was now officially an aggressor in its longest war, which lasted until 1975, after American troops withdrew and the Vietcong army captured Saigon.

During the course of the war, the USA used chemical weapons on North Vietnamese targets. One of these was **AGENT ORANGE** which was designed to kill off plant life, forcing farmers who supported the Vietcong to leave the region as well as depriving the Vietcong of cover. Five million acres of forest and millions of acres of crops were destroyed. It is claimed 400,000 were killed or maimed by this toxic chemical and the a million people in Vietnam today have health problems stemming from Agent Orange. In addition, the My Lai Massacre in 1968 involved a company of US infantry who killed, raped and mutilated the inhabitants of a village they suspected was loyal to the Vietcong. Massacres were also carried out by Vietnamese troops (such as Binh Tai, 1966) and by Vietcong troops (such as Dak Son, 1967).

Does the American aggression in Vietnam demonstrate **JUS AD BELLUM**? The USA was trying to stop Communism spreading throughout Asia, but Just War Theory specifically disallows starting a war for political purposes. The Just Cause has to be self-defence or a necessary pre-emptive strike or an intervention to save innocents. None of these three conditions applies. The Vietcong did not attack America or pose a threat to America and the reprisals after the attack on Camp Holloway contravene Jus In Bello as well.

Another justification is that American troops were rescuing the South from being invaded by the Communist North. The problem with this is that the southern government the USA was protecting was an illegitimate one that had fixed elections and lost the support of its people. It was only American fire power that kept this regime going. Supporting an illegitimate regime against the will of its own people is not Just Cause.

Things are not much better when we consider **JUS IN BELLO**. The key ideas here are Right Intentions and Proportionality. It is legitimate to support one side in a civil war if it is outgunned by the other, but only to balance the fight. This sort of intervention was used in Libya in 2011 when UK and US airstrikes helped the rebels defeat the well-trained and well-equipped army of Colonel Gaddafi. This was not the case in Vietnam, where the US forces tried to defeat the Vietcong in battle, not just restore the balance of power. Of course, the atrocities show that none of the sides discriminated between combatants and innocent civilians.

Finally, we must consider **JUS POST BELLUM**. The departure of American forces and the collapse of the corrupt South Vietnamese government led to many more massacres. Many tried to flee the country to escape the Vietcong and it is estimated that 12 million people became refugees as a result of the war. Half a million fled by sea and it is estimated 10-15% of these died and the survivors struggled to be allowed to settle in new countries. Vietnam, even once unified, was ruined: its farmland was poisoned by chemicals, its population reduced and it remains one of the world's poorest countries. The Communist Vietnamese government today continues to suppress dissent and religious freedom and mistreat ethnic minorities.

However, not everyone interprets the Vietnam War in this way.

To some supporters, resisting Communism in Asia was a Just Cause. Communism did not exist when Thomas Aquinas developed Just War Theory, but some argue that its oppressive and totalitarian nature is evil. According to this view, fighting a war to stop Communism is not the same as fighting a war for political reasons.

The Gulf of Tonkin Resolution was passed by Congress in 1964 so this gave the American forces Legitimate Authority to fight.

Although the American war effort failed, it was believed at the time that a bombing campaign would force the Vietcong to surrender or negotiate, so there seemed to be Probability of Success.

Negotiations, partitions and elections had been tried all through the 1950s and 1960s but they had failed, so American intervention was a Last Resort.

Although massacres took place and cover-ups were attempted, the USA did arrest and court martial the leaders of Charlie Company for their part in the My Lai Massacre and the commanding officer, Lt. Calley, was convicted. The Pentagon set up the Vietnam War Crimes Working Group to investigate all atrocities and discovered 320 cases, including prisoners being tortured, and 57 soldiers faced court martial. This could be evidence for Discrimination and Right Intention.

The US Government set up Humanitarian Operation to assist the refugees escaping from Vietnam. 823,000 settled in the USA itself. Although US-Vietnam relations were broken off after the war, since the 1990s the USA started giving aid to Vietnam, especially for the war wounded, and now gives at least $50 million a year in aid. This goes some way towards Jus Post Bellum.

DEONTOLOGY AND JUST WAR

Deontology seems to fit more comfortably with Militarism or Pacifism than with Just War Theory. This is because a person might feel they have a duty to fight for their country or a moral law against killing, but Just War Theory claims war is a necessary evil and it can never be a duty or a law to do something evil.

However, Deontology in ethics is rather more sophisticated than this. Even though there may never be a duty to fight and kill, a Deontologist will admit there are duties to do other things, like protecting innocents or restoring justice. What happens in war is that different duties or moral imperatives come into conflict, such as the moral rule that says killing is wrong and the rule that says protecting yourself or saving others is right.

One way of resolving this that has already been considered is the Doctrine of Double Effect (**DDE**), which is popular with Catholic ethicists and supporters of Natural Law Theory.

Another famous Deontologist is Immanuel Kant and he also arrived at a moral acceptance of war similar in many ways to Just War Theory. The essence of Kant's moral thinking is the good will, which is very similar to the idea of Right Intention that guides Jus In Bello.

However, Kant is also concerned with the idea of universalising our values - if I claim that what I do is right, I must be prepared for it to be right for everyone to do it. On the face of it, you can't universalise the idea that killing people is right, particularly mass killing. This leads to a contradiction in will (because you couldn't seriously wish for a world where everybody killed everybody else) and a contradiction in nature (because such a state of affairs would wipe out the human race). More generally, war is all about using people as a means to an end - generals use their soldiers as a means to hurt the enemy, bombers use civilian casualties as a means to make the enemy surrender. War seems pretty far removed from a Kantian ethic.

Nevertheless, Kant approved of war under certain conditions. He took a pessimistic view of humanity (the **TRAGIC VISION** described by Stephen Pinker and illustrated by Thomas Hobbes) and viewed war as inevitable. He then universalised the idea that people have a right to defend themselves, creating a moral principle that we can go to war when we are threatened.

This view is actually closer to Defencism or Pacificism than it is to Just War Theory but there is another aspect of Kant's thought that is closely in line with Just War thinking. We can also universalise the idea that we should go to the aid of others when they are threatened (because we'd want others to help us out if the situation were reversed). In fact, if people only ever fought to protect themselves or protect an innocent, then no one would need to fight at all, which is the logical goal of Kantian ethics.

Kant (1795) is also very influential in the development of Jus Post Bellum, which he calls "Right After War". Kant argues that the object in war is:

> *"To constrain the nations mutually to pass from this state of war and to found a common constitution establishing perpetual peace."*

In other words, peace is the goal of war and war becomes unjust the moment we lose sight of this. Kant particularly singles out, as the sort of strategies that might win a war:

> *"... the employment of assassins, poisoners, breach of capitulation, and incitement to treason."*

But he condemns these strategies as making a lasting peace impossible, thereby making the war unjust.

As a student of philosophy, you will need to consider whether you share Kant's pessimism about a world without war and if so, whether his concern with establishing lasting peace is misguided or an important moral insight.

AGAPE AND JUST WAR

Agape is selfless love, but this is not the same as "warm fuzzy feelings". A person can act on Agape even while they are causing pain or even killing someone, such as a surgeon. St Augustine of Hippo, who first proposed Just War Theory for Christians, argued that Agape means you must do everything in your power to protect or rescue an innocent person, even if that means using force.

This idea of Agape as something rather hard-nosed and compatible with war was the main inspiration for Paul Ramsey, an American philosopher who adapted Just War Theory for Protestant Christians. Ramsey (1968) argues that Agape involves seeking to protect others, even when that brings risk to yourself. This pretty closely describes what soldiers do in war. Ramsey argues that we should all be non-resisting Pacifists when it comes to one-on-one problems. If you are being mugged or threatened personally you should "turn the other cheek" as Jesus taught. Ramsey's view is that, in a straight choice between loving your attacker and loving yourself, you should choose to love your attacker and this means refusing to use violence against them.

However, Ramsey thinks ethics work differently in "multilateral relations", which is where one group of people is trying to harm another group of people. In situations like this, Agape means we have to place more importance on loving the innocent people who need rescuing than in loving the attackers who are endangering them. Agape is the sort of love that is prepared to kill so long as the motive is selfless.

Interestingly, Ramsey extends this thinking to nuclear deterrence. Ramsey was writing during the Cold War, when America and her allies believed the threat of nuclear war prevented the Soviet Union from conquering Europe. This, according to Ramsey, is Agape.

A critic might ask, if Agape is compatible with launching a nuclear attack, what is Agape not compatible with? This leads to the main problem with Agapeic thinking about Just War. Agape, philosophers like Ramsey insist, is not to be confused with the sentimental, emotion "love" of everyday language. It is something different, more intellectual, more concerned with the will and motives for acting. But when Agape is used to justify turning half a continent into a radioactive wasteland, it seems as though Agape has become so different from ordinary "love" that it hardly deserves to be called "love" at all. In fact, it doesn't seem any different from "hate".

As a student of philosophy, you will need to decide for yourself whether Agape can mean anything at all in the context of Ramsey's "multilateral relations" and the destructive power of modern warfare.

TELEOLOGY AND JUST WAR

Just War Theory is in many ways completely opposed to the Consequentialist view of war. A war is considered Just if it fits certain characteristics (ordered by a legitimate authority, last resort, proportionate force and so on) or if it has certain motivations (a just cause, right intentions). Consequentialists in ethics will completely reject this sort of approach.

One problem with Just War Theory, from a Consequentialist viewpoint, is that once a war is Just it becomes the right thing to do, regardless of its consequences. This can easily produce arrogance or self-righteousness. Leaders may feel that, since the war is Just, it would actually be morally wrong to negotiate with the enemy, offer a truce or accept a conditional surrender. For example, at the end of the Second World War the Allies demanded Nazi Germany's unconditional surrender; the Nazis refused and so the war dragged on to a bloody battle for Berlin. A controversial view is that, if the Allies had been prepared to accept a conditional surrender (perhaps one that left the Nazis in power but with a different leader), a lot of lives might have been saved.

Consequentialists reject the idea that something can be right and just purely because it fulfils a set of conditions or has a certain motivation. Instead, they argue it is the consequences that make something right or wrong. For example, Utilitarians focus on maximising happiness for everyone concerned. This is a very flexible view. A Consequentialist will regard a war as Just as long as it is producing justice as an outcome (or at least, more justice than any of the other options available). Once the consequences start looking unjust, then the war is no longer a Just War.

This viewpoint might be much closer what happens in actual wars, which often start with one set of motives or objectives, but then have to change part of the way through. For example, the US-led invasion of Afghanistan in 2001 started off as a way to prevent Al-Qaeda from launching any more terrorist attacks. However, soldiers stayed on in Afghanistan for over a decade fighting a Taliban-led insurgency against the new Afghan government. In 2011, President Obama announced the US troops would start withdrawing from Afghanistan. From a Consequentialist viewpoint, withdrawing would do more good than staying on, despite the appearance of being "defeated".

This Consequentialist approach to war creates different problems. With Just War Theory, soldiers can know whether the war they are fighting is just or not and what sort of things would change it into an Unjust War. On the other hand, we can only know in hindsight, after the war is over, whether it led to just consequences or not. This makes it difficult to accuse soldiers or governments of War Crimes. In order to blame somebody for something, they had to know it was wrong at the time they did it. Most soldiers and generals are well aware of the moral rules of warfare (such as the Geneva Conventions), but very few soldiers can foresee the way a war turns out. For example, President Truman's decision to atom bomb Japanese cities in 1945 was followed swiftly by the surrender of Japan so only a minority of people today think of him as a war criminal; if Japan had fought on in spite of the bombings, more people might think of the bombings as a war crime because they didn't accomplish anything good.

This is a problem with Consequentialist ethics generally, but it applies particularly strongly in the case of war the consequences in war are very uncertain and the stakes are so high.

As a student of philosophy, you will need to decide for yourself whether wars can be just or unjust based purely on their consequences. Are there things that must always be excused? Or lines that can never be crossed?

ARETE AND JUST WAR

According to Virtue Ethics, one of the Cardinal Virtues is Justice. Therefore a virtuous person will certainly want to know if a war is compatible with justice, if it will correct an injustice, make a society more just or even help the people who fight in it to become more just.

Just War Theory answers these questions by insisting that war has a Just Cause, if it considers Comparative Justice for both sides and even if it leads to Jus Post Bellum.

The idea of war making soldiers into better people is more closely linked with Militarism. Just War Theory starts with the assumption that war is a necessary evil, not a mixed blessing. If war is evil, people are not morally improved by it except in the general way that everyone who suffers any sort of evil can be improved (by becoming more patient, forgiving, appreciative, and so on).

However, viewing war in terms of Arete also encourages us to think about how war can reveal the moral character of the countries involved. Thomas Jefferson (1787) wrote about revolutions:

> *"The tree of liberty must be watered from time to time with the blood of patriots and tyrants."*

Jefferson seems to be saying that one of the key things about a good society is that it is prepared to fight to defend its freedom and perhaps extend those freedoms to others.

In contrast, an unjust society can make all sorts of excuses for itself during peace time, but in war its injustices are made clear for everyone to see.

One example from World War II was the Japanese "kamikaze" attack. The Japanese pilots flew fighters called Zeros which were very fast and manoeuvrable because they had no armour protection for the pilots. Japanese pilots often were not provided with parachutes. Such "luxuries" were thought to disgrace the warrior code of Bushido. Some were even sent out without enough fuel to return home: when their fuel ran out they were supposed to crash their plane into an American ship.

Also during World War II, the Russian Marshal Zhukov asked why the Americans fed German prisoners the same rations as American soldiers. President Eisenhower replied that if the German soldiers were badly treated, the Nazis might treat captured Allied soldiers badly in return (classic Realist thinking at work). Zhukov was supposedly puzzled by this: "Why do you care about men the Germans have captured? They have surrendered and cannot fight any more." Zhukov also ordered Soviet troops to march across minefields as a way of clearing mines, saying: "Our infantry attacks exactly as if it were not there."

Both of these examples reveal a callousness and a disregard for the safety of individual soldiers, opposed by Just War Theory. It is also opposed by Arete, which insists that a society must be just and treat its members justly and this becomes more important, not less, when the society is put to the test by war. In war, a society must behave virtuously or else it ceases to be a society worth fighting to preserve.

Critics might say that all societies behave equally badly in war. Is what Zhukov or the Japanese did in World War II any different from generals commanding British infantry to cross No Man's Land and attack enemy trenches in World War I? Or the blanket bombing of Dresden and the atomic bombing of Japanese cities in World War II? It's a very common piece of wartime propaganda that "our side" behaves decently but "the enemy" acts dishonourably.

As a student of philosophy, you will have to decide yourself whether it is important for a society to conduct itself virtuously in war, even if this leads to losing the war, or whether the important thing is to win the war in any way possible, even if this makes it hard for a virtuous society to exist afterwards.

CHRISTIANITY AND JUST WAR

Although Christianity did not invent Just War Theory, Christian writers like Augustine of Hippo and Thomas Aquinas developed it and gave it its philosophical credentials. The Christian pessimistic view, that this is a Fallen World where evil is inevitable, helped shape the view of war as a necessary evil, rejecting the Realist view that it is necessary only to win it.

Another example of Christian thinking about war is made clear by this example:

> On February 7, 1943, submarine captain Howard Gilmore was on routine patrol in the South Pacific when he encountered a Japanese ship and was forced to ram it. The submarine suffered great damage and came under heavy fire from the Japanese ship's machine guns. Gilmore was outside on the observation tower with two other seamen. They were killed and Gilmore was badly wounded. Despite the protests of his officers and crew, he ordered the submarine to dive without him inside it. The submarine escaped and the 69 men in the crew survived, but Howard Gilmore died on the surface. He was posthumously awarded the Congressional Medal of Honour.

Of course, Christians are not the only ones who can show this sort of courage but the point is the emotion of awe we feel when we hear about this sort of heroic self-sacrifice. Despite the horror and tragedy of war, many examples emerge of something that seems greater and some writers refer to as "transcendence" - the ability of ordinary people to show superhuman levels of bravery, selflessness and integrity.

For Christians, this self-giving sacrifice is modelled by Jesus, who explained it to his disciples:

> "My command is this: Love each other as I have loved you. Greater love has no one than this: to lay down one's life for one's friends. You are my friends if you do what I command. I no longer call you servants, because a servant does not know his master's business. Instead, I have called you friends, for everything that I learned from my Father I have made known to you." (John 12:15)

For Christians, the ability of humans to show this sort of self-sacrificing love is a pointer to the activity of God in human lives. In behaving this way, Christians most closely imitate Christ and share in his triumph over sin and death, even though they die in war themselves.

Moreover, Christians believe that wars will be a part of human history until the Second Coming:

> "You will hear of wars and rumours of wars, but see to it that you are not alarmed. Such things must happen, but the end is still to come. Nation will rise against nation, and kingdom against kingdom." (Matthew 24: 6-7)

With this in mind, many Christians reject Pacifism because they regard a world without war as impossible. Instead they try to find ways to imitate Christ within war, turning experiences of fear and suffering into opportunities for transcendence.

If you are studying philosophy from a Christian perspective, you will need to decide for yourself whether the idea of "transcendence" is a serious moral goal for Christians or just a sentimental reaction to sad stories. The idea that God can be active in a special way during war, if true, will have implications for other areas of Christian thought, such as the Problem of Evil.

THE JUST WAR THEORIST'S LETTER OF LAST RESORT

If the British Prime Minister were a Just War Theorist, what instruction would they put in the Letter of Last Resort?

Nuclear weapons have posed a problem for Just War Theory since in 1945. The Catholic Bishops of America rejected them as immoral but fell short of condemning the policy of nuclear deterrence.

Obviously, a Just War cannot be a war of revenge. That would not have Right Intention. Normally, nuclear attack would not be Proportionate either, but in this scenario, with Britain destroyed, nuclear retaliation would be proportionate. The retaliation might not be based on revenge either. As we explored in the chapter on Pacifism, for deterrence to work other countries must believe, with 100% certainty, that it will be used against them. If the submarines do not retaliate, then the nuclear deterrence used by other countries (who may so far have survived the war that destroyed Britain) will become ineffective as deterrents. This makes it more likely nuclear weapons will be used again in the future.

A different problem with the ethics of retaliation is that it makes Jus Post Bellum incredibly difficult to achieve. A nuclear attack wipes out a population and poisons a landscape, with effects that last for generations. Pope John Paul II (1983) spelled out the immoral consequences of using nuclear weapons:

> *"Any nuclear war would inevitably cause death, disease and suffering of pandemonic proportions and without the possibility of effective medical intervention … As a people we must refuse to legitimate the idea of nuclear war."*

Nonetheless, in this scenario a nuclear war has already taken place, whether it was legitimate or not. The British Prime Minister is now the "legitimate authority" and might think that Comparative Justice (based on what the enemy has done to Britain) and Right Intention (based on the threat such an enemy poses to the world and the diminishing power of nuclear deterrence if the retaliation is not launched) would justify launching the missiles.

There is an irony here for us to consider. Militarists and Realists would probably not fire the missiles, Pacifists certainly wouldn't. The only ethical position that is seriously considering telling the submarine captains to retaliate with nuclear weapons is the Just War Theorist. The ethical philosophy based on Christian love and the protection of innocents is seriously considering firing nuclear missiles.

This paradox is at the heart of what many critics find so disturbing about Just War Theory. Despite its high principles and religious origins, Just War Theory can be used to justify acts of war that other philosophies, even Militarists and amoral Realists, would reject. This is because, in defining war as a necessary evil, Just War Theory suggests that evil things can be necessary and therefore justifiable. So some critics believe Just War is a dangerous idea and a corruption of Christian ethics.

It's important to note that we haven't concluded that a Prime Minister acting on Just War Theory would certainly order retaliation. Only that such a Prime Minister would have to consider it as a moral option. An important feature of a Just War is that it meets all the criterion for justice, ad-, in- and post-. The Challenge of Peace (1983) emphasises that a Just War must be winnable. In the scenario we are considering, Britain has already lost, which might mean the moral course of action is to surrender or run away, but never to fight on.

KEY TERMS

- **COMPARATIVE JUSTICE**

- **DISCRIMINATION**

- **DOUBLE EFFECT**

- **JUS AD BELLUM**

- **JUS IN BELLO**

- **JUS POST BELLUM**

- **JUST WAR**

- **LEGITIMATE AUTHORITY**

- **NECESSARY EVIL**

- **PRE-EMPTIVE**

- **PROPORTIONALITY**

- **RIGHT INTENTION**

SELF-ASSESSMENT QUESTIONS

1. Explain what is morally necessary about war.

2. What is the difference between Jus Ad Bellum and Just In Bello?

3. Outline the strengths and weaknesses of Just War Theory.

4. What would be a Just War Theory interpretation of a conflict in the world today?

5. Is it true that no war ever qualifies as a Just War?

6. What are the problems with discriminating between combatants and innocents in modern wars?

7. Why do we have moral obligations towards the losing side in a war? Does this apply even if they were the aggressor? Does it apply to Nazis?

8. How could you win a war in a way that makes lasting peace unlikely? Why might this be immoral?

9. Can a nuclear war ever be a Just War?

10. Is Just War Theory a betrayal of Christian conscience?

FURTHER READING

- **DOWER, N** - The Ethics of War & Peace (2009), Polity, Ch 4

- **FIALA, A** - Practical Pacifism (2008), Algora, Ch 3-4

- **OREND, B** - Ethics, Killing & War (1995), Cambridge, Ch 4-5

- **OREND, B** - The Morality of War (2006), Broadview, Ch 1-7

- **TEICHMAN, J** - Pacifism & The Just War (1986), Blackwell

- **WALTZER, M** - Just & Unjust Wars (1977), Basic Books

Postscript

Jonathan Rowe received an MA in English Literature and Philosophy from St Andrews University. He qualified as an English teacher in 1992 but since 2002 has been teaching Psychology, Sociology and Religious Studies at Spalding Grammar School in Lincolnshire.

He is a great fan of Virtue Ethics, especially as practised by Beowulf, and shares the taste of most eudaimonists for rock music, jazz, real ale and Fantasy Role-Playing Games (FRPGs). He's edited hobby magazines and published short stories and is delighted to be writing for PushMe Press.